What people are saying about ...

LESSONS FROM THE EAST

"Bob Roberts is absolutely right about our need to reimagine the church as a people-movement reaching into all the domains of society. And so few in our time have earned the right to deliver this message with such authority as he has. This is a genuinely prophetic book; we do well to heed Bob's advice."

Alan Hirsch, founder of 100 Movements, Future
Travelers, and Forge Mission Training Network
and author of several award-winning books

"Bob Roberts Jr.'s latest book, *Lessons from the East,* is the mature fruit of a dynamic global ministry and hard-earned wisdom. Many people write about the global church, but few write from personal experience like Bob. This book is a spiritual and strategic feast! I wish this book had been available when I was a young pastor. Chapters 'The Public Square' and 'Engaging Other Faiths' are immensely practical and urgently needed in the multicultural, multireligious world in which we live. This is a must read for every pastor in the West."

Rick Love, PhD, president of Peace
Catalyst International and author of
Grace and Truth and *Peace Catalysts*

"This is a brave and important book. It deserves, no demands, the widest readership and flagship status as one of the timeliest and highest conversations on the church's horizon."

Leonard Sweet, bestselling author of
From Tablet to Table, professor, and
architect of preachthestory.com

"Bob Roberts is the Indiana Jones of Christianity! He is a one-of-a-kind leader and follower of Jesus. Listen to him. He has, on a personal basis, seen how Jesus is moving around the world in spectacular ways. Will you let him teach you? Now be warned, he is going to wreck your grid. Then like a master builder, he will rebuild something more beautiful, something more gospel-centered and powerful in your life than you can imagine."

Derwin L. Gray, pastor of Transformation
Church and author of *The High Definition Leader*

"Over the decades Bob and I have known each other, I've seen Bob's sense of humor, winsome ways, and love for people develop into a sage-like wisdom. And thank God Bob hasn't lost his divinely gifted mischievous ways that cause him to see things differently. He has been awakened to more gifts, like cultural adaptation and relational development, that he shares with us in his book *Lessons from the East*. I think every church leader in America should read this. I rarely say stuff like that, but this is a must read for how to reframe doing church in a global community. It's a taking off of an old garment and donning a new one perfectly fit for where we are as a church now. *Lessons from the East* is a welcome addition to the body of work that Bob has written to help us engage cross culturally with a Texas-size heart of love. Buy the book for you and all the leaders in your church. It's worth the investment."

Dave Gibbons, author of *Xealots*
and *Small Cloud Rising*

"Bob Roberts has traveled the world and interacted with leaders from a variety of cultures and backgrounds. The lessons he has learned and what he shares will enlighten you, empower you, and encourage you."

John Jenkins, author and senior pastor
of First Baptist Church of Glenarden

"There is no one I trust more than Bob Roberts to help me navigate the complexities of East meets West with clarity, confidence, and compassion. He is experientially engaged, relationally connected, and greatly respected by diverse others here in the United States and around the globe. As such, he is well positioned and can be trusted to help you and your church adapt to a changing world for the sake of the gospel."

Dr. Mark DeYmaz, pastor of Mosaic
Church of Central Arkansas, president of
Mosaix Global Network, and author of
Leading a Healthy Multi-Ethnic Church

LESSONS
from the
EAST

Also by Bob Roberts Jr.

Transformation
Glocalization
The Multiplying Church
Real-Time Connections
Bold as Love
A Field Guide for Everyday Mission
(with Ben Connelly)

LESSONS *from the* EAST

FINDING THE FUTURE
OF WESTERN CHRISTIANITY
IN THE GLOBAL CHURCH

BOB ROBERTS *Jr.*

LESSONS FROM THE EAST
Published by David C Cook
4050 Lee Vance View
Colorado Springs, CO 80918 U.S.A.

David C Cook Distribution Canada
55 Woodslee Avenue, Paris, Ontario, Canada N3L 3E5

David C Cook U.K., Kingsway Communications
Eastbourne, East Sussex BN23 6NT, England

The graphic circle C logo is a registered trademark of David C Cook.

The website addresses recommended throughout this book are offered as a
resource to you. These websites are not intended in any way to be or imply an
endorsement on the part of David C Cook, nor do we vouch for their content.

LCCN 2016930111
ISBN 978-0-7814-1376-3
eISBN 978-0-7814-1430-2

© 2016 Bob Roberts Jr.
Published in association with the literary and marketing
agency of C. Grant & Company, Wheaton, Illinois.

The Team: Tim Peterson, Alice Crider, Amy Konyndyk,
Jack Campbell, Susan Murdock
Cover Design: Nick Lee
Cover Photo: Shutterstock

Printed in the United States of America
First Edition 2016

1 2 3 4 5 6 7 8 9 10

020216

I want to dedicate this book to my
daughter, Christina Jill King.
No father could be prouder or more grateful
for his daughter than I am of you.
I am in awe of your
call,
gifts,
character, and
ministry.

My encouragement to you is to
love God with all your being
and
love others with the entirety of your
head, heart, and hands.

CONTENTS

PART III KINGDOM ACTION

Introduction

A NEW WAY TO SEE

I'm just a country boy from East Texas. If my high school annual had featured a page for "Least Likely to Travel the World," you'd have found my picture there. And if I ever left our shores, I'd have been "Most Likely" to look for a Dairy Queen instead of exploring and enjoying the culture.

But God had other plans. Through a series of unplanned, unforeseen events, God connected me with the most remarkable church leaders I've ever known—leaders from the far corners of the globe. God has used these people to inspire me and challenge me, to give me a far bigger vision and a tenderized heart for people. Amazingly, these remarkable leaders don't see themselves as anything special.

My relationship with them has opened my eyes to see things—in me, in my church, and in our culture—that I'd never even noticed before.

THE NEED FOR CHANGE

These leaders have shown me a deep and tragic flaw in the way American pastors usually think. We believe our chief contribution to society is putting on attractive worship services. It's not. We can be successful in attracting people to these gatherings yet not make much of a dent in their hearts or improve their effectiveness as Christians. The primary benefit we offer our communities (or we can offer if we try) is creative, selfless, tenacious service. If we put our efforts there, a lot more people will wonder what's different about these people who love others so much. We build credibility in our communities by serving people outside our walls with no strings attached. But we severely limit our influence by our self-promotion, competition, and disdain for those who are different from us.

I know a lot of pastors. Many of those in America are looking for the silver bullet to make their churches excel. They go to conferences and read books and articles to find "the key" to increase attendance or have the most dynamic worship services. American pastors are desperately searching for the missing links that will turn their churches into incredible successes—but many of them are asking the wrong questions and searching for the wrong answers.

I know because I was just like them. For decades, my heroes were the big-name pastors who had grown enormous churches and who now hold conferences to tell all the rest of us how to be just as successful. But I haven't been. I learned a lot of important and helpful principles from these pastors, but when I met the global pastors, I saw something categorically different. These leaders have a different purpose, a different mind-set, a different strategy, and a different level of humility. As soon as I met each one, I said, "This is what I want to become! This is what I've been longing for, but I didn't have the words to describe it!" They live the gospel all week, not just on Sunday. They make a difference in every domain in their communities; they don't wait for people to come to them. And they see the power of the Holy Spirit radically and unmistakably change lives. To them, all of this is completely normal. I wanted it to be normal for me too. Gradually, thank God, it's happening in my life.

The American church doesn't need one more silver bullet. We need a surgeon to cut us open, perform radical surgery on our hearts and minds, and then empower us to be and do all God has for us. I've talked to a lot of wonderful young pastors who are terribly frustrated. At least some of them are waiting to arrive at some level of success so they can feel significant, and they assume their purpose in life is to strive like crazy to get there. When they discover they can live in the moment in the power of the Spirit, serve gladly in the public square, think small and multiply, it's like a ten-ton weight has been lifted off their shoulders. They can do that, and they can do it now!

Actually, I believe the Holy Spirit is calling us—and has been calling us—to the kind of life and ministry I've seen in my friends overseas. Most of us just haven't been listening. Or perhaps the noise of the American church has drowned out the voice of the Spirit. I didn't hear him very clearly for a long, long time, but I'm starting to hear him better now—and it's the greatest thrill of my life!

An accurate diagnosis is the beginning, but it isn't enough to bring healing and health. As the Spirit renews our love for God and refreshes our calling to love God and people, we are no longer at cross-purposes with the Holy Spirit. We begin to cooperate with him instead of using him to make us successful (and blaming him when we aren't). In many ways, the message of this book is wrapped around three transformations in my life:

- discovering and pursuing the kingdom of God through kindness, justice, and righteousness instead of my success;
- engaging the world—learning from global leaders about faith in God and caring for the world's people—instead of being consumed with growing my church; and
- listening to the Holy Spirit instead of assuming I know how to make life and ministry work.

The American church excels in celebrating what goes on inside the walls of our churches, but our country—and our culture—is becoming increasingly pluralistic, diverse, and secular. In response, the church too often is seen as either angry or irrelevant, or both. Pastors on the other side of the world have lived with pluralism and diversity for generations, but few are in cultures that are becoming as secularized as ours. They've learned how to relate to the people in their communities, especially those who have very different beliefs, political opinions, and ethnic backgrounds. They've learned how to attract people to the beauty and truth of Jesus Christ instead of becoming marginalized.

From 1492 to 1792, from Christopher Columbus to Captain Cook, the Age of Exploration opened the doors for foreign missions. For the last two hundred years, the world has seen an explosion of

Christianity in the areas where no Christians were known. During this time, the Western church in Europe and North America poured blood, sweat, heart, and tangible resources into the rest of the world. We saw amazing results. We are now entering an era I call the "Great Exchange," in which those of us in the West become the students and global pastors are our teachers. Today, a few churches in America are growing, and many are declining. Overall, evangelicals are barely holding their own. We won't grow, we won't thrive, unless we find the humility to learn from leaders who are seeing God do amazing things in the most difficult places on earth.

Virtually all observers have commented that the American church is, to a significant degree, broken and unhealthy. In his book *The Great Evangelical Recession*, John Dickerson made stark and alarming predictions. He offered practical (and urgent) steps to avoid the recession, or at least to prepare for it. But Dickerson isn't the only voice of warning. At many conferences, we hear prophetic voices pleading for the church in the United States to return to her first love. But maybe our search for answers is too limited. Could the solution lie outside our borders? Do we have something to learn from the vibrant, growing, powerful global church? I believe we have a lot to learn from leaders beyond our shores! One of our main tasks at NorthWood is to absorb the principles we're learning from the global pastors and contextualize them. We aren't the biggest or the fastest-growing church in our area, but we've engaged our city, our nation, and several other nations of the world. We've multiplied to over two hundred churches, and God is doing incredible things to build his kingdom among us and through us. It's humbling and thrilling to see God use us in this way.

I've been in the room with several of these global pastors when American pastors arrive to teach their strategies, share their resources, and promise to serve them in different ways. The global pastors are very courteous and grateful for the offers, but the Americans seem to be speaking a different language—literally and figuratively. The global pastors never insist they're right or they have the secret. They humbly serve, love, and minister for God and his kingdom instead of trying to build their reputations, and they trust the Spirit's power because they realize they're sunk without him.

If we'll listen to these leaders, we'll learn life-changing truths about God's kingdom and power. If we'll go there, we'll see gentle, courageous men and women—whose lives exemplify the Lamb of God and the Lion of Judah—making an impact on their communities as the foundation of church planting. They build credibility through selfless service and gracious declarations of God's truth, not by self-promotion, and not by complaining and attacking when they don't get their way. At every point, they give away their power to rising leaders. And they're thrilled about every person who is trusting God to make a difference in their corner of their communities.

I'm not trying to paint too rosy a picture of these global leaders. They experience tremendous stress, but theirs seems to be categorically different from the professional stress many American pastors suffer. Our stress is often related to comparison, competition, and the deep disappointment that our churches aren't growing as we hoped they'd grow. This kind of stress creates divisions, resentments, family breakdowns, and burnout. The type of tension the global pastors experience is more like "compassion fatigue." They feel the burden of their people's poverty, sickness, and life-threatening political and military situations. But I've also seen far more joy, peace, laughter, hope, and love among the global leaders. Their commitment to God's kingdom instead of their own and their trust in the Spirit's power instead of their own free them, to a great degree, from the oppression of comparison and competition.

I meet with these twenty-six men at least once a year. Each time, it's the very best family reunion. We're so glad to see each other, but the first thing we do is get on our knees together to pray, thanking God for all he is to us and all he's done for us. This isn't a perfunctory prayer to begin a meeting. We pray without a clock, as long as we want or need to pray, fully abandoned to the Lord's will and ways, pouring out our hearts in praise and asking God to work miracles in the toughest situations back in our cities. No one is in a hurry, and no one has to be prompted to pray. There is such reverence for God and respect for each other. These times of prayer are the highlights of my year, and then I get to spend a couple of days with men who have become my best friends.

MY HOPE FOR YOU

Pastor or church leader, I want to assure you that you are far more valuable to God and his kingdom than you ever imagined. You don't have to wait until you run a megachurch to change the world. You can do it now, today, right where you are with the resources God has already put in your hands. World-changing revival seldom comes through megachurches, but through megamen and megawomen who listen to the voice of the Spirit and do what he tells them to do. Megachurches aren't the model in the New Testament, in the early church, or in thriving churches in all parts of the world today. Sure, they offer an incredible array of resources and do a lot of good, but they aren't the best models to build multiplying disciples. From Neil Cole to Alex McManus, and from Alan Hirsch to Jeff Vanderstelt, all of them are taking church to the neighborhood, the workplace, the school, and wherever people do life. They think big instead of small. If you're the leader of a small church, you already have an advantage. Use it.

But you'll almost certainly have to change your mind-set about life and ministry. Keeping the same strategy and trying harder won't work. There's a different way, the way I'm learning from the pastors I've met from the far corners of the globe. If you aren't a megachurch pastor, you aren't second class. In fact, you're the best hope for God and his kingdom. You're more flexible than Rick Warren, Tim Keller, and Matt Chandler. You're in a position to shift gears more easily to serve in the domains in your community, to decentralize power and authority, and to multiply disciples so your community and the world are reached with the message of the gospel.

The hope of the American church (and the world) isn't in the hands of a few hundred pastors of megachurches but in the hearts and hands of the 460,000 pastors who have been called by God to love him with all their hearts, serve with selfless joy, love the unlovable, and pour into the lives of men and women who will multiply themselves into other leaders and other churches. If you're one of these leaders, you matter. You're in a place to learn from the incredible pastors who have taught me so much in the past few years. In the chapters of this book, I'll tell you about them and the lessons I've learned from them.

Part I

KINGDOM VISION
AND STRATEGY

Chapter 1

WHAT ARE WE MISSING?

Church leaders have been praying for revival in America, and we've been working hard to help our churches grow, but we're falling behind. The Pew Research Center reports that between 2007 and 2014, the number of people who claimed to be Christians dropped almost 8 percent. In light of this decline, we might be encouraged to learn that those who identified themselves as evangelicals fell less than 1 percent.[1]

Outside our borders, however, Jesus is capturing hearts and the church is exploding, especially in Africa, Asia, and South America. For instance, in 1900, Africa had only 8.7 million Christians, but today, the number is almost 400 million,[2] and some estimates are half a billion. In Korea, the number of Christians has grown from 2 percent in 1945 to 30 percent today.[3] The Pentecostal movement is barely a hundred years old, but it has grown at an astonishing rate. Today, one in twelve people alive today has some form of faith defined by Pentecostalism.[4]

For years, American church leaders assumed we were the experts, we had the right theology and strategy, and we had all the resources we and the rest of the world needed. We've conducted an incredible array of conferences and seminars on how to lead and manage our churches. The problem is that we have a closed system. We've been searching for answers from each other, but not from outside our borders. We've sent missionaries and resources overseas, but we haven't listened to the leaders from those countries. In the meantime, the American church has become stagnant while the global church is seeing phenomenal growth. Church leaders on other continents are leaving us in the dust. The solution? We've been givers, but now it's time to become receivers. We have a lot to learn—from them, not from each other.

In my lifetime the United States has shifted from being the most prolific nation in the world in sending missionaries to being the third most unreached nation in the world. When I first became a pastor, I didn't realize that I'd become a missionary by *staying in America* instead of *leaving America* for a distant land.

Because we now live in a mission field, we need to learn from the experts: our global sisters and brothers. Western Christians have exported Christianity to the ends of the earth. Ladies and gentlemen, it's time to import! We need to be discipled by pastors from the nations where the church is exploding. To learn from them, we need a healthy dose of humility. Oh, we want to reach our nation for Jesus, but we don't want anyone telling us how. We need a different perspective: missions isn't something one part of the church imposes on another part; instead, it's something we do together, humbling ourselves before one another.

If we don't change, we're setting ourselves up for a crisis. We need to stop looking at the world as "our mission field" and see it as a global community, a global church with global answers—answers even for us.

Let me draw a few contrasts between the American church and the church in much of the rest of the world:

- In America, we're fighting to keep our church attendance from declining, but the church in many parts of the world is growing far faster than the birthrate.
- In America, we excel at systems and processes, conferences and seminars; overseas, church leaders have fewer resources and organizational systems, but they have far stronger relationships.
- In America, discipleship is a process people generally learn in a classroom; overseas, imparting spiritual life, values, and heart is a way of life.
- In America, we've taken the separation of church and state to the extreme so that many Christians seldom mention their faith outside the walls of their churches. Overseas, believers are often in the minority, so they don't take their faith for granted. They're light and salt in every domain of their lives: at home and at work, in their communities and in their churches.
- In America, many believers are skeptical of culture and often stand back to criticize government, schools, and every other aspect of society. Overseas, Christians are more engaged with these arenas—not as antagonists, but as allies.
- In America, church is designed to entertain the people who attend so they'll come back the next

week; overseas, the purpose of worship is to encounter the living God.

- In America, we assume we can't have a movement of God without pure and perfect theology. In other parts of the world, leaders are far more interested in an authentic relationship with Jesus that radicalizes a person's life. They fine-tune their theology as the relationship grows stronger and deeper. In other words, they don't start with doctrine. They begin with the relationship with Jesus and then let the richness of the relationship define the doctrine.

- In America, pastors hope (secretly or openly) to be celebrities, and they compare themselves to those who have made it big. But in the rest of the world, some of the finest leaders I've ever known gladly labor for Christ in obscurity. Humility is the hallmark of their lives.

- In America, we know very little of real opposition, threats, and suffering. In many parts of the world, pastors and their followers live with these challenges. Real danger produces a more robust faith.

- In America, we often compete with each other for acclaim and attendance (the conversion rate is abysmally small, so most growth in churches is from sheep swapping), but overseas, pastors often serve at the risk of their lives, so they are very supportive of one another.

- In America, megachurches are growing rapidly at
the expense of the neighborhood churches. Since
1990, the number of megachurches has increased
by 1,600 percent.[5] Overseas, decentralization is
the key to growth at every level: for individuals,
small groups, and small churches. They seldom
build huge worship centers. Instead, they continue to multiply small congregations where
relationships are strengthened and deepened.

Obviously, I'm making broad, but accurate, generalizations in
these contrasts, as well as in all the contrasts I'm drawing throughout
the book. There are, of course, many exceptions to these observations,
but the patterns are clear. These descriptions aren't merely academic
theories or philosophical assumptions. I've seen the difference. I
have the privilege of calling more than two dozen amazing leaders
from around the world my friends. All of us are church planters
because multiplying leaders and churches runs in our blood. These
amazing leaders think small and multiply. One of them has planted
churches that have an attendance of over a million people. Others
have networks of cells and congregations numbering in the hundreds
of thousands. These aren't megachurch pastors; they're gigachurch
pastors! We call our gathering the Global Collaborative Community,
and we meet twice a year. Most are from the East—Asia, the Middle
East, and Africa—but a few are from Europe, Central America, and
South America. Only two Americans are in the group. I'll tell much
more about these remarkable leaders to illustrate particular points in
this book, but for now let me introduce you to a few of them.

Eddy Leo is the pastor of Abba Love Church in Jakarta, Indonesia. This is a different kind of megachurch. It has had about thirty locations, providing about seventy services. Recently, it divided into ten independent but connected churches. These congregations are spread all over the city of ten million people. A few years ago, a number of psychologists met with Eddy, and together they heard the whisper of the Spirit inviting them to care for people in the city who were homeless and mentally ill—"the least of these" if there ever were any. They began a church *for* people who are mentally ill, *with* people who are mentally ill, and *of* people who are mentally ill. Today, the church that was birthed out of caring for people living on the streets has grown to about two thousand.

Joseph Maisha has a church of seventeen thousand in the predominately Muslim area of Mombasa, Kenya. They have also planted 110 churches throughout the country. His church sponsors a full array of social services for the community, including schools, a college, orphanages, and leadership training for people in business and government.

Jossy Chacko is a successful businessman who lives in Melbourne, Australia. Originally from India, Jossy converted from Orthodox to Protestant, and he realized God had put him in position to make a difference in his native land. He has planted thousands of churches by selecting visionary leaders, giving them each a bicycle, and telling them to begin by serving their communities. Today, this network of small churches includes more than two hundred thousand people.

Dion Robert is a pastor of a church of 250,000 in the Ivory Coast of West Africa. During a political coup and resulting conflict, his church became a hospital to care for the wounded from both sides. Other pastors might have been afraid of being accused of taking sides, but Dion solved the problem with a powerful blend of personal strength, inclusive grace, and tangible medical care. Do you think people in the country heard about his church? Do you think they were amazed at the love demonstrated to those who had tried to kill each other just moments earlier? Do you think his church is now positioned to be a powerful force for reconciliation in that troubled land?

For all of these leaders—and the rest of my friends who are like them—the goal isn't to build big churches, and their strategy isn't to make their worship services the most attractive in their cities. Their goal is to make multiplying disciples, and their strategy is to serve selflessly in the places where unbelievers live and work, see whose heart God touches with the gospel, and then start a gathering of believers who believe community involvement, evangelism, and deep relational connections are the heart and soul of the Christian life. To them, everything is about the multiplication of small, heartwarming, difference-making units.

As I've gotten to know these remarkable leaders, I've realized their churches aren't growing because of their systems, processes, marketing, or expertise. What they're *doing* isn't as important as *who* they are and *how* they serve. Their compassionate hearts, strong values, and humble service enable them to lead in a way that multiplies their vibrant faith in God.

THREE EXPRESSIONS

In Acts and the New Testament letters, we see three distinct expressions of the church: the cell, the congregation, and the universal church. In his letter to the Ephesians, Paul explains that the role of leaders is to help people "attain to the unity of the faith and of the knowledge of the Son of God, to mature manhood, to the measure of the stature of the fullness of Christ, so that we may no longer be children, tossed to and fro by the waves and carried about by every wind of doctrine, by human cunning, by craftiness in deceitful schemes. Rather, speaking the truth in love, we are to grow up in every way into him who is the head, into Christ, from whom the whole body, joined and held together by every joint with which it is equipped, when each part is working properly, makes the body grow so that it builds itself up in love" (Eph. 4:13–16). How does this kind of growth happen? Not by sitting side by side in a worship service, but in the give-and-take of dynamic relationships in which people love one another, forgive one another, accept one another, rebuke one another, and encourage one another. This can happen only at the level of cells of about four to a dozen people.

The congregation is the expression of the body of Christ where cells gather for teaching, training, direction, and vision. Together, they strategically engage the city and, as light and salt, penetrate each domain of influence in the community. Cells are often comprised of people with similar backgrounds, but congregations are made up of very diverse cells. For instance, Joshua Vjaykumar faces the challenge of reaching people in all the castes in his state in India. He says that if he created a church only for the upper castes, those in the lower castes wouldn't come, and if he planted a church primarily for the lower castes, people in the upper castes would stay away. To resolve this seemingly intractable problem, he has created cells designed for each caste, and then the cells come together as a very diverse, unified congregation. With this strategy, his network has baptized more than twenty thousand people of all castes in their communities. If God can use Joshua to create a diverse but unified congregation among the hard lines of the caste system in India, I believe God can do it anywhere—even in your city.

The global church, the "universal church," is the body of Christ around the world in many different expressions but with a single purpose of bringing glory to God. When we love and serve with humility, we learn from one another. But when we believe we are superior or inferior, we miss the blessing of being a strong, united body. Sadly, the global church isn't even on the radar for most American church leaders. If they mention the "universal church" at all, the hearers are often left with a vague concept of all denominations sharing some kind of mystical union. They don't have a genuine grasp of the robust power, creative wisdom, and vibrant spiritual life exhibited in congregations all over the world—power, wisdom, and life that could inspire and direct the American church.

In 2015, I spoke at the Exponential Conferences for eight thousand church planters in Tampa, Florida, and Newport Beach, California. As I explained the principles I'm learning from my friends across the world, the lights came on for many of the people in the room. A number of them came up to me after my session to say, "This is so encouraging! I'm the pastor of a small church, and I can still make a difference. I thought I had to compete with Darrin Patrick, Matt Chandler, Tim Keller, Rick Warren, Tommy Barnett, Andy Stanley, and Bill Hybels. Now I realize a few people who understand kingdom principles can change their city. My church can make a difference, now!"

At the conference, the planners provided a small room for a breakout session for a small group of church planters on how small churches make a big difference. The room had sixty chairs, but over one hundred people crammed into the back and sides. Kevin Cox, an American pastor who is implementing these principles, led the group. He shared that his church was six years old, with about 180 in weekly attendance, but they had started fourteen churches. As he talked, every eye was riveted on him, and every person in the room "wanted to be that guy"!

I called on another American pastor, Scott Venable, to share his story. He too is implementing the principles both of us have learned from overseas. His church near Chicago was four years old, with sixty people. They've already planted eight churches.

By their own admission, these leaders aren't the sharpest tools in the shed. In many ways, they're just like me—thoroughly average, except the fact that they have a very different ministry model than most pastors in our country. They're engaging the domains of their communities—education, business, medicine, entertainment, technology, economics, and government—serving selflessly, not to *do* evangelism, but to *be* Christ's loving hands, feet, and voice. Out of the relationships they form and credibility they earn in this work, people hear the gospel and trust in Christ. At some point, new believers gather in a cell, and as cells gather, the church begins. But the people in these cells have a very different DNA from those in most churches in America. They believe Christians are engaged in their communities—because that's how they were engaged. They believe relationships are more important than flashy programs, because that's how they got involved. And they believe the power of cells is where dynamic growth happens, because that's all they've ever known about church. It's a very different way of thinking about church.

THE LEARNING COMMUNITY

In 2008, I met with six other pastors from around the world to talk about what we could learn from one another. In the years since then, we've been very selective about who we invite to join us. The Global Collaborative Community now includes twenty-six of us. As we've seen how Eddy teaches, trains, and involves believers in Jakarta, we've adopted his discipleship model of cell churches. Jossy is a businessman, not a pastor; but he has led churches at different points in his life. All of us have learned valuable organizational principles from him. His insights about systems, processes, and leader building have transformed our understanding of how networks function. A pastor from England, Terry Virgo, has taught us that people aren't consumers and we're not promoters; we're all part of the family of God, so believers should relate to one another like a loving, honest, supportive, fully engaged family. In Kenya, Joseph Maisha has learned how to relate to people who come to Christ from other religions.

In America, especially in the South and the Midwest, most people have a Christian heritage. That's not true in much of the world, particularly in Muslim areas. Joseph has taught us to engage with love and truth, not truth and suspicion or truth and hate—or despising people so much that we don't share the truth with them at all. Joseph has learned to share the gospel of grace without enraging the local Muslim leaders. Actually, he has become friends with many of them. His diplomatic skills are equaled only by his incredible ability to communicate the gospel clearly and powerfully. A pastor in China has taught us that church planting isn't a specialized professional vocation; it's the normal expression of every heart devoted to Christ and those who love people in their communities.

DOMAINS

All of these leaders were already involved in the public domain, which can be described as the infrastructure of a society. When I've talked about the domains found in every community, some people have asked, "What exactly do you mean?" Some authorities identify three realms: business, civil society (such as schools and medical care), and governance. I think it's helpful to point to more categories. The following diagram illustrates eight primary domains within a given society, each with several examples of careers.

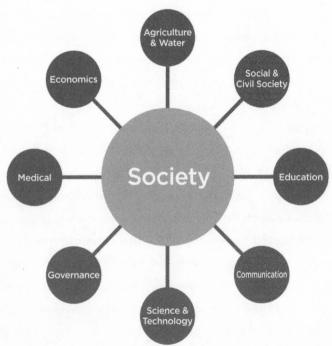

You might look at the diagram and ask, "Where's the church?" The church is present in every domain of society as disciples live, love, and serve there. When the church is considered a separate domain, it becomes isolated from the rest of society. When this happens, the church becomes marginalized as one of many competing voices instead of God's people living powerfully and lovingly in every domain of society. Also, when the church is a domain, often it is viewed primarily as a political force and God's people are seen as narrow, angry, and demanding. This, of course, further marginalizes the credibility of the church.

God has given us a bigger, broader, deeper purpose than carving out a single domain. The task of the church is to make disciples who engage the broad context of society for the kingdom of God to be increasingly realized on earth. We don't establish God's kingdom "on earth as it is in heaven" by remaining separated and marginalized. We take steps to make the kingdom a reality in our world by living for Christ in every domain in our society, in the love and power of the Holy Spirit, not by the manipulative, strong-armed methods of the world.

The global pastors intentionally equip their people to live, work, and serve in the domains of their communities. They conduct after-school programs, provide services for the mentally ill, meet with government officials to promote the welfare of citizens, and serve in many other ways. Jossy established sewing centers for people to make garments and earn a living. Eddy asked barbers and hairdressers to teach people who were mentally ill to cut hair so they could make a contribution to society. Joseph started orphanages for kids who lost their parents to AIDS.

In these and countless other types of involvement in the public domain, these leaders met people where they live, work, and learn; became trusted friends; shared the gospel; and formed cells in the context of caring and serving. And the people in the cells have multiplied their faith, their service, and their love in the lives of others.

CONSIDER THIS

What do you think of the assessment of the American church in this chapter? What do you agree with? What comments seem out of proportion?

What statements in this chapter bother you? Which ones inspire you?

As you learn more about the global church, what do you hope will change in your heart, your church, and your church's impact on your community and the world?

Chapter 2

A BIGGER PICTURE

From Church Focused to Kingdom Focused

When you ask Christians in America to define and describe the "kingdom of God," you often hear one of two answers. Some say it means "Jesus lives and rules in our hearts." Others have a more distant view; they explain that it refers to the millennial kingdom when Jesus returns to rule on earth. Both of these are true, but they have a missing middle. In many of his books, New Testament scholar N. T. Wright explained that the kingdom of God was "decisively launched" at the death, burial, and resurrection of Christ and that it will be fully consummated in the *palingenesia*, the renewal of all things in the new heaven and new earth. Today, Jesus is seated at the right hand of God in the place of authority. We live squarely in between the inauguration and the complete fulfillment of his rule. Our calling—the calling of all Christians—is to act, love, and serve today so God works through us to answer our prayer, "Your kingdom come, your will be done, on earth as it is in heaven" (Matt. 6:10).

After Jesus faced Satan and the temptations in the wilderness, he returned to Nazareth. On a Sabbath, he was handed the scroll of Isaiah. He unrolled it and found the place where he read:

> The Spirit of the Lord is upon me,
>> because he has anointed me
>> to proclaim good news to the poor.
> He has sent me to proclaim liberty to the captives
>> and recovering of sight to the blind,
>> to set at liberty those who are oppressed,
> to proclaim the year of the Lord's favor.

Jesus rolled up the scroll, handed it back to the attendant, and sat down. As every eye fixed on him, he announced, "Today this Scripture has been fulfilled in your hearing" (Luke 4:18–19, 21). The kingdom of God, Jesus was saying, exists by the gracious acts of the king to proclaim good news, to liberate those in bondage, to heal the sick, and to bring social justice to the distressed in the community. If we follow the king, that's our calling too.

The problem, of course, is that many of us don't live like Jesus is our sovereign, majestic, wise king. We're not alone. The earliest Christians needed to be reminded again and again. In *How God Became King*, Wright explained:

> The story the gospels tell, of a Jesus who embod-
> ied the living God of Israel and whose cross and
> resurrection really did inaugurate the kingdom of
> that God, remained not only incomprehensible,

but unheard. The New Testament writers did their best to make it heard and to make it understood. Matthew believed that Jesus had already accomplished it: "All authority," declares Matthew's Jesus, "in heaven and on earth has been given to me" (Matt. 28:18). Paul believed Jesus was already reigning; you can't understand Romans or 1 Corinthians or Philippians unless you take that as basic.[1]

A few years ago at a large conference of pastors from around the world, I sat with two men, Eddy Leo and Sam Sung Kim. It was my introduction to these remarkable leaders. Eddy is a pastor in the largest Muslim country in the world, Indonesia, and Sam Sung started a church in a very repressive country in Central Asia. They live thousands of miles apart, but they came to the same conclusion about the kingdom of God. They realized God wants all believers to make a difference in their communities.

There is no "upper story" of pastors and "lower story" of the rest. All believers are called, all are ministers, and all can have an impact on the people around them. We may be doctors or farmers, plumbers or executives, teachers or housewives, pastors or city council members, but all of us follow the king and represent him through our words and actions.

As Eddy thought and prayed about the kingdom of God, he wondered what it would look like for the people in his church to have a radical impact on their city. A businessman bought land and started a plantation to grow lettuce. He invited street kids who had no hope to come there. Many of these kids were orphans, and others had run away from home. The man patiently taught them how to work with discipline and excellence. This plantation grows the lettuce used in the McDonald's restaurants in Indonesia.

I've already shared the story of the medical professionals who were moved to care for the mentally ill living on the streets of Jakarta. Instead of lobbying the government to care for them, Eddy and the psychologists created a place for them, treated them with respect, and taught them the skill of cutting hair so they could earn money and live with dignity. Many of these men and women came to Christ. The congregation is called the Crazy People Church. They wear this badge with honor.

These and the other global pastors aren't devoted to building a church; they're devoted to building God's kingdom on earth. They don't just teach about God's love and power; they demonstrate it in very tangible ways. They proclaim the good news, but only after they've won the right to be heard by providing medical and social services to the community—not just for the Christians in the community, but for everyone in need.

THE KINGDOM DAWNS

I was a little slow to understand the meaning of the kingdom. For years as a pastor, I was obsessed with growing a big church. I desperately wanted to be the next Rick Warren. I admired him so much. (To be honest, I *envied* him so much.) I understood and taught the gospel of salvation and the principles of growing a big church, but I was miserable.

In my drive to grow, we moved our church to a better location. Church-growth experts assured me we'd grow by 30 percent in the first few months. We didn't. We declined. I was deeply discouraged. After a particularly terrible Sunday, I went home discouraged. The next morning, I walked to a hill near our house. I wanted to quit. I complained to God and blamed him for not coming through. Suddenly, the question filled my heart: *Bob, when will Jesus be enough for you?*

The question rocked my world because I instantly realized he *wasn't* enough for me. If he were, I wouldn't be so miserable, I wouldn't be so competitive, and I wouldn't stake my reputation on numerical success. Instead, I would be satisfied—no, I'd be thrilled to know the love of Christ that surpasses understanding!

Immediately, I responded, "God, not my empire, but your kingdom. From now on, it's about you and not me." Instantly, two things happened: First, I stopped thinking like a pastor who was focused on building a church, and I started thinking like a missionary who had a far bigger, wider, deeper vision of ministry. A church-focused pastor asks, "How's my church?" A kingdom-focused missionary asks, "How's my city?" I realized a lot of large, wealthy churches exist in cities where people suffer staggering problems. These churches may be fortresses where Christians feel safe, but often they aren't salt to preserve the dying and make the gospel tasty, and they aren't light to illumine the darkness in individuals, families, and cities.

For three years, I focused my studies on the kingdom of God. It's a big deal. In fact, it's the message of Jesus and about Jesus in the Gospels. Matthew begins with Jesus's birth, and then John the Baptist appears as the predicted forerunner preparing the way of the Lord. To everyone who will listen, he announces, "Repent, for the kingdom is at hand." John baptizes Jesus, and then Jesus goes into the wilderness for forty days. When he comes back, he works miracles as signs that the kingdom has come. He calls his apostles and tells parables to explain the kingdom. After the resurrection, he meets with the apostles for forty days to explain the kingdom again (and again). The kingdom of God, it seems, was a really big deal for Jesus and the apostles; it should be a big deal for us as well.

Second, I began to realize that living for the king meant shaping my life by the Sermon on the Mount. It makes a difference—a big difference. Recently, I attended a conference in New York at the Council on Foreign Relations. At the event, I met a philosophy professor from India. We went to the airport together, as we had the same flight out of New York. In the gate area, we had a wonderful conversation about the meaning of life. I asked him about Hinduism, and he asked me about my faith. At one point, he asked, "Bob, what is the essence of the Christian life?"

Instead of answering, I asked him, "You're a very observant person. How would you answer that question?"

Before he could respond, I remembered that Gandhi had answered the same question. When I reminded him of this, he laughed and said, "Yes, he said the essence of the Christian life is the Sermon on the Mount." I nodded, and then he asked, "But, Bob, can you show me any Christians who live that way?"

I tried to explain: "The key to living by the kingdom is that it's always a work in progress for every believer. And the lessons of Jesus's sermon have to be applied specifically in each situation." I reminded the professor what E. Stanley Jones said: Gandhi did more good with his partial understanding of the gospel than most Christians do with a full understanding. Jones became a good friend to the Mahatma, and at one point in their relationship, he asked, "Mr. Gandhi, though you quote the words of Christ often, why is [it] that you appear to so adamantly reject becoming his follower?"

Gandhi answered, "Oh, I don't reject Christ. I love Christ. It's just that so many of you Christians are so unlike Christ. If Christians would really live according to the teachings of Christ, as found in the Bible, all of India would be Christian today."[2]

Gandhi meditated on the Gospels, particularly the Sermon on the Mount, for two hours each day. Though he was a Hindu, Jesus's teaching was the foundation for all of his efforts as the leader of reform in India. A few years ago, I spoke at an event in Boerne, Switzerland, for five hundred world leaders, sponsored by the Swiss Foreign Ministry. Raj Gandhi, the great leader's grandson, was also on the program. I asked him if the story about his grandfather's commitment to reading the Bible were true. He smiled and said, "Yes, it's absolutely true." He stopped for a second and then said, "And I read it too. Bob, there's something incredible about the kingdom of God."

I had to ask myself: If Jesus's teaching about the kingdom of God, understood and lived out by a man who wasn't a Christian, transformed the subcontinent of India, why isn't it changing us? The message of Christ is far more than "ask Jesus into your heart, go to church, be a good person, and you'll go to heaven when you die." It's about being radically transformed so that we profoundly impact our communities. It's about God's rule and reign, not someday, but *this* day as we patiently and assertively love and serve people in the power of the Holy Spirit. I'm haunted and stimulated by two questions about the kingdom: Is the seed of the gospel planted in a person's heart strong enough to transform the person's desires, attitudes, and behavior? And is the seed of the gospel planted in a community strong enough to radically transform the life of that community?

I had so narrowed the gospel to "saving souls and the promise of heaven" that I completely missed the reality of the presence and power of Christ to change lives and whole communities today. But no longer. The kingdom was dawning on me.

SAVED TO GO

When we read the Gospels, we realize the kingdom is central to the message of Jesus. Our Savior is our king. When he ascended to the right hand of the throne of God, it wasn't to abandon us to our own devices. He is seated at the place of authority where he rules. Just as Jesus began the kingdom work he announced in his first sermon in Nazareth, he modeled it in healing the sick, feeding the hungry, restoring sight to the blind, and releasing the captives by paying the price for sin they couldn't pay. And when he ascended, he promised to send the Holy Spirit to work in us and through us to continue and expand the same work of the kingdom. He appointed us to be his ambassadors. The mandate hasn't changed, but it has spread; it has gone beyond the borders of Palestine to the whole world.

The message of the Bible is "Repent and believe the gospel." Some people are horrible sinners who have done unspeakable things. Thankfully, no sin is so great that it can't be forgiven by the sacrifice of Christ. But others are so prideful that they don't think they need to be forgiven. They need to realize their pride is their chief sin before a holy God. For all of us, younger believers and elder believers, hated tax collectors and arrogant Pharisees, the gospel gives us a new way to relate to God. But justification isn't the end of the story. We are partners with God to make his rule more of a reality on earth. He is both loving Savior and mighty king. All who repent and believe are indwelled by the Holy Spirit. We're adopted into the royal family. We no longer need a priest to mediate for us. We're all priests who go to God on behalf of our neighbors in the community.

Paul pronounced his grand understanding of the kingdom in his letter to the Colossians. He wrote:

> [Christ] is the image of the invisible God, the firstborn of all creation. For by him all things were created, in heaven and on earth, visible and invisible, whether thrones or dominions or rulers or authorities—all things were created through him and for him. And he is before all things, and in him all things hold together. And he is the head of the body, the church. He is the beginning, the firstborn from the dead, that in everything he might be preeminent. For in him all the fullness of God was pleased to dwell, and through him to reconcile to himself all things, whether on earth or in heaven, making peace by the blood of his cross. (Col. 1:15–20)

Who is our king? He is the creator of everything in the universe. Many believers, including pastors, have such a small view of Christ.

We often think of him as a little bigger and more powerful than us, like Superman or one of the Avengers. He's more than that—much more. If the distance from the earth to the sun, about ninety-three million miles, is represented by a piece of paper, the distance to Alpha Centauri, the nearest star system to our solar system, would require a stack of paper seventy feet tall. And the distance of the diameter of our galaxy would take a stack 310 miles high![3] And our galaxy is only one of about two hundred billion like it in the universe. The Hubble telescope has enabled us to see billions of stars and galaxies, but that's not all there is to God's creation. Scientists now tell us that the physical world we can see is only a small fraction of the mass of the universe. There is far more "dark matter" than visible matter. Jesus is the creator of all we can see *and* all we can't see, the stars and the dark matter, and the domains in every community as well as the invisible angelic and demonic powers at work to control or undermine them. Everything, from the elements of the desk where I'm sitting to the atoms of the farthest star in the heavens, was created by him, through him, and for him. So our questions should be:

> How are the schools in our community giving glory
> to the risen king?
> How are the businesses representing his interests?
> How is medical care being given to those who can't
> afford it?
> How are the arts reflecting God's creativity?
> How is the government a force for kindness, justice,
> and righteousness on earth, the qualities that delight
> God (see Jer. 9:23–24)?

These domains don't give glory to God out of a vacuum. They honor God as his people serve with integrity, work with joy, and patiently love others in each part of the community. Our mistake in America is that we've shown up in these areas, especially the schools and government, demanding our way instead of serving selflessly. When we don't get our way, we complain even louder as we walk out the door and disengage. Instead of being salt and light, we've become tasteless and dark. Sinners were attracted to Jesus, but many of them despise us. There must be something wrong. We've made faith its own isolated domain where we can hide from the world, but it was never meant to be a separate domain. Faithful, loving believers are to live and work in every domain to be "blameless and innocent, children of God without blemish in the midst of a crooked and twisted generation, among whom you shine as lights in the world, holding fast to the word of life" (Phil. 2:15–16).

Paul explained to the Colossians that Jesus is the head of the church. He is the "firstborn from the dead," which is the promise that we also will experience resurrection. In Jesus the fullness of God is found. What is his purpose? Not to grow big churches, but to reconcile all things to himself—all things on earth and all things in heaven; all domains everywhere—by the humble, sacrificial love he displayed on the cross, which transforms us into humble, creative, enthusiastic, bold servants in our communities.

The kingdom of God, Paul taught us, is fully embodied in the life and ministry of Jesus. And as we follow him, we have the unspeakable privilege of being his partners in the greatest adventure of all time: reconciling all things—people, domains, and authorities—under the loving, powerful rule of Jesus Christ.

In America, people who trust in Christ often see the church as a haven away from the evils in the culture. Jesus (and Paul, Peter, John, and the rest of the early church leaders) saw salvation as an opportunity to be a chosen, adopted, forgiven disciple *within* the web of relationships, business, and institutional connections.

Who receives the gospel of the kingdom? Who is honored to be God's partner in reconciling all things? Flawed people like you and me. We don't wait until God has finished transforming us before we engage the culture and make a difference. We engage people in our domains *as we are being* transformed. People see the changes, and they're amazed!

In the American church, we often think of classroom instruction as the primary ingredient of discipleship. Classes can impart knowledge, but the true benchmark of a disciple isn't right doctrine or ministry strategy; it's attitudes and behaviors being transformed by the Spirit of God. As individuals are being transformed by the power of God, they live out the principles of the kingdom, and their communities are gradually transformed.

A vision of the kingdom requires creativity, compassion, and flexibility. A few years ago, Ministry of Education officials in Vietnam asked me to find a Christian university in America to sponsor and staff a school in their country. The government offered to provide land and buildings. They insisted, however, that some of their professors teach in the school and lecture on communism and different views of God. I was really excited about this incredible opportunity to have an impact on the top level of leadership in that country. But when I came back to the United States and met with Christian college presidents around the country, not a single one was willing to sign on. With one voice, they all said, "We can't have any professors at our university who aren't Christians. And we can't teach curriculum that's not biblical."

In each conversation, I responded, "Why not? How can we be salt and light if we aren't engaged with decay and darkness? Why are we afraid to have opposing views presented? Are we afraid our God and our truth won't stand up to the tests?"

I'm afraid we don't really believe the gospel of the kingdom. If we did, we wouldn't react in fear and arrogance. We wouldn't retreat when we don't get our way. We'd find every opportunity to embrace the lost and the least instead of seeing them as projects or protecting ourselves from them. We'd enter the most desperate parts of our communities to humbly serve and listen to show we care. We'd wonder why our churches are monochromatic instead of multiethnic, but we're too busy growing our churches and defending our turf to engage the community and expand the kingdom.

Jesus wasn't criticized for his rigid views on cultural issues. Quite the reverse. He was hated because he loved the people others despised. In the same way, the measure of how much the kingdom has taken root in our lives is the extremity of our love for misfits and outcasts, the down-and-outers and the up-and-comers, the pitiful and the powerful, the people who annoy us and those who can't stand us. Jesus loved widows and orphans, who were at the bottom of his society's ladder of respect, and he loved Samaritans, lepers, and sick people who were considered unclean. He didn't wait for them to come to him. He took the initiative to enter their world, to spend time with them and get to know them. They delighted in experiencing his great love, but the religious leaders hated him for loving those they despised.

Who are "those people" in my world? Do I despise Muslims, gays, rednecks, addicts, inner-city young black men, people on welfare, or undocumented immigrants (to name some of the most common ones)? Or do I at least tolerate them and muster just enough civility to have guarded conversations with them? Or do I go where they are to get to know them, listen to them, and love them enough so they feel comfortable with me? And here's the big one: Do any of them call me their friend?

Not long ago I was in New York at an event. When it was over, I walked out to the sidewalk to get a cab to the airport. A woman who had also attended was waiting nearby for a cab. That day, she had spoken up for the LGBT community and talked about her church. Christians don't have a very good reputation with that community because we don't know how to present our truth with grace and love. Too often we come across as narrow and angry. I wanted the opportunity to represent Jesus to her and treat her with respect. I wanted her to know that even if we disagree, she's valuable to God and to me.

When a cab pulled up, a friend and I were next in line. Instead of jumping in and ignoring the woman, I turned and asked if she was going to LaGuardia Airport. She said, "Yes."

I said, "Please ride with my friend and me."

She smiled and nodded. I took her bags and put them in the trunk, and I held the door for her as she climbed in. When I got in, I introduced myself and told her I had heard her talk that day, and I asked her to tell me more about her church. She explained that her church was growing really fast and it was predominately comprised of gay Catholics and evangelicals. Two gay pastors had planted the church, one from a Pentecostal background and the other a Southern Baptist.

She looked very curious as to why I would be interested. For her, something wasn't connecting. I told her, "You and I may disagree about the theological teaching about homosexuality, but I respect you as a person. And one more thing: there's never any justification for treating anyone with disrespect."

She sighed and told me, "Bob, thank you for telling me that."

I had been wrestling with some problems in our church related to this issue, and I suddenly realized she was exactly the right person to ask for advice. I explained, "We have had families in our church whose kids have become involved in homosexual lifestyles. What would you advise me to tell these parents?"

She smiled. "Oh, Bob, that's easy. I wish more pastors would ask me questions like that. I'd advise the parents to communicate three things: I love you; you're always going to be part of our family, no matter what choices you make; and we're both on a journey to find out how to make this work."

She stopped for a moment and then continued, "That third one is really important. When I told my parents I'm gay, they instantly rejected me. I expected them to be perfectly fine with my decision and my announcement, but I'd been on the journey for a long time—they hadn't. I needed to give them time to go on their journey to understand me."

Her input was precisely what I needed to hear. This was a kingdom conversation. The gospel of the kingdom doesn't isolate us from people who are different from us; it connects us to them with radical, unconditional, irrational love ... and they can feel it. They probably won't drop to their knees instantly and repent in dust and ashes, but they'll be more likely to listen to us when we lovingly tell them—again—about Jesus.

The kingdom perspective isn't optional overseas. It's standard operating procedure. If pastors around the world don't connect with people in love, respect, integrity, and honor, they may get killed. And in fact, they may be killed anyway. Most, if not all, of the global pastors I've come to know are in countries where Christians are in the minority. I believe the best way to learn to be kingdom focused is to be a member of a minority in a culture. Since the Pilgrims set foot on Plymouth Rock, American Christians haven't been a minority in our land, but it's happening today. Many of us are fighting like crazy to avoid the slide instead of using the changes in our culture as a golden opportunity to show the love of Jesus to everyone who's watching. My friends overseas never act like victims or bullies. They've learned to represent Jesus in every domain in their communities. They've built friendships with those who agree with their worldview as well as those who don't.

TRIBES

The biggest threat to the kingdom of God isn't liberal politics or bad theology; it's tribalism. I'm not talking about headhunters in Borneo. I'm talking about the tendency of people to gather with their own kind and reject anyone who doesn't conform to their beliefs and standards. We can form isolated tribes according to ethnicity, religion, nationality, class, gender, economic status, politics, loyalty to a football team, and almost anything else we can imagine. Wherever

you see walls of suspicion and rejection of others, you'll find an identifiable tribe behind the walls.

In tribes, people listen to their leader more than they listen to
the Spirit of God. The accepted dogma of tribes creates superiority
and suspicion: we're right, and if you disagree, you must be wrong.
Tribes, by definition, isolate and divide instead of breaking down
walls and building bridges.

Not everything about tribes is bad and wrong. They give people
a sense of identity and belonging, but it's a poor substitute for the
greater identity as God's beloved child and belonging to a kingdom-
minded community.

My friends in the East have a very different view of "missions."
Too often in the recent past, missions has described Americans or
Western Europeans traveling to foreign lands to plant churches as
outposts of American church culture and strategy. Volumes have
been written and courses have been taught about making these
churches culturally relevant without diluting the truth of the Bible.
But I have another concern. Too often, our emphasis on missions has
been more about *creating a separate domain* than *equipping people to
enter the existing domains* in those communities to shine as lights and
love people the way Jesus loved. At its worst, missions has been about
religious colonialization, but the kingdom is about the renewal of all
things. If you noticed the domain chart in chapter 1, you saw that
church wasn't one of the domains—this is very important!

Though we can't see him, the king isn't AWOL. He's present
and ruling now. Eddy Leo observed, "Christ rules today through
his body, the church. To extend his reign, we need to expand his
body." Christ's kingdom is very messy, with endless varieties of

expressions and many setbacks, but it's in this mess that he wants us to live and serve. He has given us a task to do, and he honors us by calling us his friends and partners. We aren't agents of religion or agents of church growth. We're the king's men and women, freely forgiven, imputed with Christ's own righteousness, full of honor and challenged by the task of being his ambassadors to reconcile all things to him.

NOTHING LESS THAN THIS

Today, many people are talking about the gospel. It's a wonderful thing to focus on the amazing grace of Jesus. I'm 100 percent for this, and I believe we need to be as clear and powerful as possible to help people grasp the good news. The sweeping message of the Bible, the good news Paul described to the Colossians, consists of four movements: creation, fall, redemption, and restoration. Too often, however, churches in the West preach a truncated gospel of only fall and redemption: Jesus died for our sins so we can go to heaven when we die. The biblical teaching of creation is that God made a good world with loving relationships and meaning-ful work, and the teaching of restoration is that those who have been redeemed are God's "workmanship," or masterpiece, "created in Christ Jesus for good works, which God prepared beforehand, that we should walk in them" (Eph. 2:10). We get a glimpse of the ultimate renewal when we see Christ resurrected, the "firstfruits" from the dead. As those who believe in the substitutionary atone-ment at the cross and the renewal of the resurrection, we play a role in the process of restoration, not just in the new heaven and new earth, but now! As kingdom people, it's our privilege to join God in taking steps to restore the world to the way he originally designed it to be. The task won't be completed in this life or this age, but Jesus has all authority, and he has commissioned us to join him in his great mission.

If we preach only fall and redemption, our people may be amazed at their forgiveness in Christ, but they won't be thrilled that God has invited us to be his partners in restoring a lost and broken world. They may do some good deeds as occasional surgical strikes, but they probably won't see themselves as God's partners to transform the domains in their communities. A truncated gospel almost certainly produces truncated discipleship, truncated passion, and truncated impact on the culture. Jesus certainly is our Savior, but he is also our great king over all.

The gospel defines God's free gift of grace, and the message of grace is our primary motivation to obey God after we believe. As leaders, we need to be sure to present the complete gospel message, one that includes the rule and reign of Christ on earth today. The grace of God justifies us, forgiving our sins and imputing the righteousness of God, and he adopts us into his family. Grace then propels us to live for the king—as we grow in his love, humility, kindness, and joy—in every domain in our lives. We've often thought of the good news applying to individuals, but the gospel of the kingdom also is good news to our schools, our businesses and our factories, our labs and our hospitals, our city councils and our art galleries. In all of these, God's people bring love, enthusiasm, creativity, and value. Grace people are (or should be) kingdom people.

CONSIDER THIS

So, which gospel are you preaching: the gospel of religion, the gospel of church growth, the gospel of your personal reputation, or the gospel of the kingdom of God?

Here's a metric to consider: What did you measure after church last Sunday? What made you feel successful and valued? What made you feel worthless and small? If your primary metrics were attendance, giving, and personal acclaim, you're building your own kingdom, and you're building it on sand. But if your main metric is people who are engaging their domains to serve and love, you're moving toward the kingdom of God.

Who is your hero? Is it the person who wrote the biggest check, or is it the one who volunteered and worked at the homeless shelter?

What did you announce from the front last week? Was it another big program that you hope will dazzle the crowd, or was it an opportunity for people to care for others?

How many ethnic groups are in your church? How does the percentage of each group in your church compare to the percentage of these groups in the community? Do people from different races and cultures feel rejected, tolerated, or warmly embraced? Do you go out of your way to get to know them? Do any of them call you their friend?

Are your people waiting for you to ask them to join your projects, or are your church's disciples innovative and excited about coming up with their own projects?

Does the gospel you're preaching include all four movements of creation, fall, redemption, and restoration? Do the people in your church exhibit a truncated identity, truncated passion, truncated mission, and truncated effectiveness?

What steps can you take to experience, teach, and model a kingdom-focused life and ministry?

Chapter 3

THE PURPOSE OF SUNDAY MORNING

From Hero Pastors to Hero Disciples

There's nothing wrong with a pastor being popular, highly respected, and honored in the community. But there's something very wrong with this pursuit being the driving force of a pastor's life. While we're on this side of the dirt, we'll have mixed motives. I understand that, but it's too easy to give in to the darker, but seemingly normal, drives of comparison and competition, measuring the wrong things and getting our identities from the wrong sources. When we delight more in *being* heroes than in *building* heroes, we've missed the heart of God and his purpose for his church.

Too often in America, we've made a successful worship service the focus of our strategy, our measuring stick, our biggest worry, and our heart's desire. In our country, we don't start churches; we start worship services. When we live according to this common yet flawed goal, we want to attract as many people as possible so we will have something to show for our efforts. And we add some programs to minister to men, women, couples, kids, and every other segment of the audience. These, we're sure, are the heart and soul of discipleship. Maybe … maybe not. If our thoughts, plans, and activities as leaders are focused on producing excellent, attractive worship services, we've missed the point. Of course, I'm not saying our goal is to produce boring, dissonant, awkward Sunday morning services, but we need to make sure our purpose is aligned with God's.

Great worship services don't change the world; empowered, impassioned disciples do. People in our communities (and people on the other side of the globe) aren't looking at the quality of our worship to see if we have something to offer them. They're looking for people who are living the heart and values of the Sermon on the Mount. Every religion has its own liturgy of worship, but only vibrant, authentic Christians live all day every day with the blend of humility and power, grace and truth. Actually, when people of other faiths (or no faith) see the disconnection between our worship on Sunday and our lives on Monday through Saturday, they assume we have nothing at all to offer them. We make a dent in their minds and hearts only if we live the gospel throughout the week—if we and our people are genuine disciples instead of showmen.

It's entirely possible, then, for a pastor and a church to have fabulous worship services but not produce community-transforming disciples. The most important metric isn't what happens for an hour or so on Sunday morning, but what happens in the homes, neighborhoods, offices, fields, and shops all week.

Why did the early church grow, and why has the church seen remarkable growth at particular periods in history? Because people in the communities saw believers experiencing the love, peace, and power of God in their daily lives—and more specifically, they saw them experiencing the reality of God during times of persecution and privation. The outsiders realized the gospel actually changes lives! I've wondered: If first-century followers of Jesus were teleported to the twenty-first century, where would they go to find the church? Would they even recognize the church? If they attended our worship, would they sense the presence, power, and love of God?

As I've gotten to know the global pastors and visited their churches, I've noticed two things: the quality of their worship services often isn't up to our standards, but the quality and number of their genuine disciples put us to shame. The "average" believers in those churches are leading people to Christ, serving in their domains, caring for the disadvantaged, and multiplying themselves in the lives of new believers. In those churches, that's not just a theory or a nice dream; it's a reality.

When I sat with Eddy Leo and Sam Sung Kim, we talked about how we made disciples. I asked both of them, "How do you do it? How do you build disciples in your churches?"

Eddy took out a piece of paper and drew a triangle. He said, "Our strategy is very simple." He drew an arrow up and explained, "*Up* is the importance of our relationship to the Father. Everything comes from him." He drew arrows from the sides to the middle and said, "*In* is how we relate to one another in loving, strong, honest relationships." He then drew arrows from the sides outward and told me, "*Out* is how we serve God in our community."

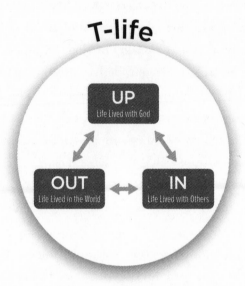

Sam Sung Kim nodded and gave his explanation, which was almost identical to Eddy's. I thought both of them were kidding me because I had written a book describing the same three directions of an authentic disciple of Jesus Christ.[1] The three of us separately had studied the Scriptures and come up with the same model. In fact, all of the pastors in the Global Collaborative Community operate using the same three simple principles. This tells me the model transcends cultural differences. It's God's model for every church leader for every disciple in every church on the planet. From St. Brendan in the sixth century to authors today such as Alan Hirsch, Michael Breen, Derwin Gray, and many others, leaders are teaching and using this ancient template.

TWO MODELS, TWO RESULTS

In my church background, the model of discipleship was "learn, grow, and go." I no longer think that's an accurate understanding of the Bible's instructions on making disciples. It's simpler than that. I believe the Scriptures tell all believers to "hear and obey." Using Eddy's triangle, we first hear from God—about his love, forgiveness, power, and purpose for us—and then we obey his voice to care for one another and those in our communities. This shifts the launchpad from "how much information a person has" to "how well a person hears the voice of God."

Sadly, we've made hearing the voice of God a rare event we pursue only for major decisions, such as who to marry and where to live and work. Instead, biblical discipleship makes hearing the voice of God normative. Of course, different traditions have different emphases and practices as they describe how we hear God, but virtually all of us accept the fact that God speaks to his children primarily through the Word of God, and also by the "still, small voice" of the Spirit's whispers, nudges, and prompting.

If the source of our spiritual lives is hearing the voice of God, the spiritual disciplines become valuable means to getting closer to God. They aren't "works" that earn anything from God. They simply provide the space and the quiet for us to be able to listen to him.

In America, we've built churches on the reputations of pastors. The brilliance of a single pastor who wows the crowd, however, was never meant to be the foundation of stability and effectiveness of the local church. The impact of the gospel is always most powerful and broad when men and women, young and old, rich and poor, of all ethnicities, are vitally connected to the Father and then love one another and their neighbors as themselves. The biblical model of evangelism isn't to bring people to church for the pastor to lead them to Christ … and then keep coming to hear him for the rest of their lives. The power of God's church isn't in the hands of a single person who is the star on Sunday morning; it's in the hands of ordinary believers equipped, empowered, and shepherded to do extraordinary things for God's kingdom.

The concept of the kingdom is empowered by the Spirit of God and grounded in the message of the Sermon on the Mount. With this power and truth we make disciples. Disciples gather into cells, and as enough cells form, a congregation emerges. In this model, the origin of a church is very different from the traditional American model, and the role of church leaders is far different. This kingdom-oriented, disciple-making DNA creates a culture of hearing and obeying, not hero worship or a program-driven ministry.

FOUR SHIFTS

As the leaders of our church have tried to apply what we've learned from our friends overseas, we've made four major shifts in our church's ministry. These overlap and interlock, but it's instructive to describe each one separately. All of them decentralize authority; they take the focus off the pastor and put the focus on the disciples.

1. From Programs to Domains

In too many American churches, people are enlisted and trained to run programs in the church instead of to be dynamic, compassionate, effective disciples where they live and work. Big churches based on hero pastors are impressive and have the resources to fund a lot of programs, but large organizations are usually too centralized and too bureaucratic to build multiplying disciples. The biblical goal isn't to produce followers whose task is to build bigger churches, but to make disciples whose primary objective is to have an impact on their domains of influence.

Kingdom-focused, domain-centered disciples use every skill and resource to have an impact on others. In one Southeast Asian country, some Christian rice farmers are moving to another country to grow rice and live lives of grace and truth in relationships with their neighbors and buyers. Their vocation is their platform for friendships and ministry.

Jossy Chacko organizes his church plants like he organizes his business interests. For him, making reproducible units is the key to his financial success as well as building disciples who replicate themselves. He identifies towns and cities where he senses God wants him to plant a church, but his first step isn't to start a worship service; it's to build a community center that offers resources to everyone in the area. The leader of the center assesses the needs in the community and provides care. The center may include an orphanage, a homeless shelter, job training, and other services. As people come to Christ in this environment, a church is birthed with the leader becoming the pastor. Jossy hires a director to oversee five community centers. And for every ten directors, he hires a supervisor.

There's a big difference in the two worlds. In America, we start churches by identifying a pastor and beginning a worship service to attract people. We provide classes to teach people about following

Jesus, but most of these people haven't seen discipleship modeled in the domains of their communities, *so they assume being a disciple means serving at the church.* As we've seen, the biblical model is quite different. Instead of creating a church that has *a program* for evangelism, the church begins with disciples *living with and loving* neighbors and coworkers. Disciples aren't made in classrooms; they're made in their relationships in their society as they listen to the voice of God and obey.

In this model, neighbors and coworkers watch the disciple's attitudes and behaviors before the unbelievers come to Christ. They see the disciple struggle with the same problems they face, but they notice the person has a source of strength, hope, and joy. In these environments, the unbeliever is learning what a kingdom-focused disciple looks like before trusting in Christ! In this way, new Christians already grasp the nature of the kingdom and the value of walking with God in domains.

2. From "Inside the Walls" to "Outside the Walls"

In the West, we bifurcate our message of the gospel and our vocations. At best, we see our jobs as platforms to share the gospel. But actually, our jobs give us an opportunity to use our abilities to create goods and services for the greater good of the community. All vocations (except those that are illegal or immoral) are valuable to God. As we work, we have the opportunity to serve people and love them. God has given us our talents and skills, and our jobs are part of our demonstration of the life of Christ in us.

I believe the primary ministry of believers doesn't happen within the walls of the church. The most important ministries of our people are their careers, in their workplaces. That's where they create value and security for individuals and families. That's where they rub shoulders with believers and unbelievers. That's where they model integrity, the righteousness and justice of God. That's where they live out the kingdom. And that's where they shine like stars in a dark and dying world. As pastors, our primary ministry is helping them see their careers this way.

If a woman is an engineer in our church, I encourage her to live for Jesus in her domain of engineering and become friends with her colleagues and clients. In natural, unforced conversations about what really matters in their lives, she can tell people what Jesus means to her. Some will become Christians, and she can start a cell of believers in her domain. That's what we now teach and model at our church, and amazingly, it happens all the time. No one needs to feel forced to do evangelism. Instead, they simply make friends with people. If they don't short-circuit their communications by cowardice or awkwardness, conversations about Jesus naturally emerge.

Like every other congregation, we have a wide range of vocations represented at our church. We have financial consultants who are disciples in their domain, artists in theirs, teachers in theirs, and plumbers in theirs. In every walk of life, our people are learning to simply live, serve, and love where they go each day, and God is using them to do amazing things. Many of our people travel around the world and connect with the domains in their fields in the cities of other countries. They've made friends by sharing their expertise, and as conversations have happened naturally, they've had the chance to lead many people to Christ. Because of them, you can find disciples in cells of artists, engineers, doctors, nurses, farmers, educators, and lots of other vocations in countries around the world.

We often forget that Paul made a living as a tentmaker during part of his ministry. When I toured the ancient city of Ephesus a few years ago, our guide was Muslim. He explained, "You Christians may think Paul was so destitute that he had to make tents so he could barely scrape by. That's not it at all. Tentmakers often made a lot of money, and besides, it was a very strategic occupation. The groups that needed tents included the Roman military, sailors who bought fabric for sails, merchants who needed tents for stalls in the market, and travelers who used them on long trips. Virtually every segment of society needed tents. Each of these was a separate group, and Paul could have used his profession to make inroads for the Christian message in each of them."

Paul told us to follow his example. We need to follow him in strategically using our vocations to build relationships and credibility in our domains for the sake of the kingdom.

3. From Controlling to Releasing

If the goal of the local church is to build a large following for the star pastor, the leaders will want to control all the programs and resources. Every activity will be measured by how it builds the pastor's reputation and the church's numbers. (The organizers probably won't talk about the pastor's reputation, but making him a star is the subtext that drives all the decisions.) However, if the goal is to advance the kingdom, God will lead the disciples to have a passion to help people around them each day. Ministry will be decentralized and vibrant … and undoubtedly messy. In a free-ranging ministry model, egos clash, preferences turn into demands, and misunderstandings cause friction. In an open culture of discipleship and ministry, problems are bound to happen. We have a choice: to keep things tidy and under control or to release people to fulfill the dreams God puts on their hearts. Of course, leaders need to give guidance so there's not too much craziness, but I believe we need to err on the side of creativity and let people soar.

If we encourage people to think, pray, and follow God's leading, they'll find all kinds of ways to serve others. One man in our church started taking meals to a couple of older people, and now he has a large and growing ministry providing food for elderly shut-ins. Some women who suffered from abuse when they were young are leading a ministry to help young women escape the sex-slave trade. An executive who suffered from neglect when he was a boy has become a mentor for fourth-grade boys. A retired executive in the medical profession and a retired, Spirit-filled pastor have teamed up to start a clinic for people who suffer from diabetes, neuropathy, and other debilitating diseases. They believe God heals through divine intervention as well as through the advances of modern medicine. God uses it all. These men have invested a ton of money in their vision, and I celebrate their vision and generosity.

When we release people to dream, pray, and serve, it's no longer the job of our church staff and board to come up with all the ideas for ministries. Our people are engaged in their domains, and they're creative enough to come up with plenty of ideas. Our job is to be traffic cops to direct people to the best paths to use their passions, talents, and expertise. We don't want to control all the traffic. We just want to limit the number of wrecks. We provide some general guidelines, but we don't feel as though we have to stay on top of every person all the time. We treat our people more like teenagers

and young adults who are growing in responsibility than like tod-
dlers who need constant supervision. By the way, smaller churches
have far more opportunities to operate as a body than large churches.
They're more personal, nimble, and creative.

If the goal of pastors and church leaders is to put on a great
service to attract people who will give generously to build even bigger
and provide more professional services, these leaders might become
successful in growing a very large church, but they will miss the point
of the kingdom. The kingdom is bottom up, not top down. It thrives
when ordinary people see God use them in their domains of work and
relationships and when they use all their creativity and compassion
to make a difference in those arenas. The job of kingdom-oriented
leaders isn't to impress them or control them; it's to celebrate them,
equip them, and release them to do even more for the glory of God.

It's very difficult to explain this concept to American pastors,
because the pressure of becoming heroes and making worship the
center of ministry is the air we breathe. Let's be honest: any society
that makes the Kardashians the top celebrities is in trouble. They're
famous only for being famous. And in the Christian subculture,
we're not much better. Many people follow celebrity pastors with
as much blind devotion as those who fawn over the Kardashians.
It's certainly not wrong to be respected for teaching God's truth
in a compelling way or building a large organization, but any
preoccupation with comparison and competition reveals a deeper,
darker motive. When our daydreams drift to our hearts' desires,
too many of us have mental images of being heroes.

While writing this chapter, I heard of another megachurch pastor who had fallen. It made me very sad. I searched the Internet to

look up fallen pastors of large churches and found dozens of cases in the past three years. Pastors are often put on pedestals that are far too high. They're human—thoroughly human. Wouldn't it be better if people saw churches as far more than their preachers? Wouldn't it be better if we weren't so enamored with celebrities in pop culture and in the church?

If, though, we will go overseas and open their eyes, we'll see a very different model of ministry in which disciples are the heroes. Of course, we can go overseas a dozen times and fail to notice the difference. Sitting on an airplane and then staying at a hotel in another country won't guarantee insight, but we can ask God to give us eyes to see what's really going on there—and then we need to ask him for the courage to radically change our model and our metrics of what constitutes a successful church. I hate to say it, but I think the people in our churches are more open to this model of ministry than most of their pastors. The pastors have a vested interest in being heroes. It's the status that's most cherished among their peers. But the people in their churches quickly grasp the revolutionary impact of every person being a priest and royal child in his or her domain. When we turn our model upside down to call disciples heroes, we turn our communities upside down for Christ.

Too often when American pastors take their people overseas, we export our church's values, strategies, and programs. They typically don't even notice what's going on in those cultures. Instead, the pastors need to take a new set of lenses to help their people see the values, strategies, and model of discipleship that already exists in the far-flung corners of the world. The believers on the other side of the world don't have the resources to compete with one another in excellence of worship services. All they have is the love they can share with their neighbors, friends, and coworkers ... but that's plenty.

4. From "For" to "With"

One of the concepts that changes how we do ministry at our church—a concept I learned from the global pastors—is that when we engage our community, we don't do things "for" them; we serve "with" them. This is how we become salt and light. When we go with a paternalistic spirit, we come across as arrogant, even if we're sacrificing time and resources to help people. When we go "with," we don't go with all the answers. In fact, we may not share any resources until we've listened enough to earn the right to be heard. This process takes time, so we don't dump resources and leave. We engage, and we stay engaged.

When we serve, we join hands with government agencies and nonprofits to provide resources, time, and attention. They may have unbelievers who run their programs, but that's fine. It only gives us another place to make friends and shine the light of God's love.

The two different models of discipleship bring us back to the original question: Who are our heroes? Are our pastors, the skilled orators who can draw a crowd, our heroes; or are the people who live for Jesus every day in their domains our heroes? A few years ago when our church turned the corner and began celebrating everyday heroes, the local media in the metroplex came to report on the story. They wanted to interview me, but I realized I wasn't the one to stand in the limelight. I pointed them to the men and women who were making a difference in their companies and their neighborhoods. They are the true heroes of the story.

CONSIDER THIS

Wouldn't it be cool if people came to your church because they were amazed at the wisdom and love of a friend instead of being amazed at your preaching or the quality of the music?

Wouldn't it be wonderful if people were drawn to Christ by friends in their domains and they'd never heard of you?

What if your biggest headache was having so many of your people creatively and passionately meeting needs in the community that they got in one another's way?

What if Sunday mornings are more about celebrating what the body of Christ is doing during the week than marketing you and the excellence of your services?

Chapter 4

FAMILY CONNECTIONS

From Sterile Institutions to Authentic Relationships

Only a generation ago, pastors and church leaders generally connected with one another through their denominations. In recent decades, however, networks that bring leaders together through common interests and goals began to emerge—and have sometimes eclipsed these ties. Denominations have been, and probably will continue to be, very important: they provide resources and support based on a shared history. When they began, they were fledgling networks of pastors with a shared vision. As they grew, however, they became institutionalized and they required a bureaucracy to support the structure, values, and resources.

Current networks, such as Willow Creek Association, Leadership Network, and Acts 29, offer vision, curricula, and connections with like-minded leaders. I've noticed, though, that most networks (for instance, those designed for planting churches) are most effective for the 20 to 30 percent of the leaders who are most closely connected to the founders. The rest are often just along for the ride, gleaning a few resources that help them, but not fully engaged.

These and other networks usually began around a common sense of mission, and then they developed a more or less consistent doctrine. As these ideas and values coalesced, the networks formed their own cultures and they became identifiable tribes. If the leaders aren't careful, they can gradually become more like bureaucratic denominations than vibrant, flexible, mission-driven networks.

My perspective isn't based on academic theory. I have personal experience. In 2000, we formed a network of churches called Glocalnet. Within a few years, it grew to about four hundred churches. The demands on me were staggering, and I realized I was acting like the leader of a denomination. That wasn't my goal at all! When we started, we generated a lot of energy and saw a lot of multiplication. As it grew larger, however, it required more energy from me and yet we saw far less effectiveness. It just wasn't working. I had to make major changes—for my sanity and to restore the primacy of mission to our relationships. When I backed away, some of my friends were surprised. I explained that God hadn't called me to be an administrative leader for hundreds of churches.

Then I met Terry Virgo. He's one of the leaders in our global gathering of pastors. Terry grew up as an Anglican in Brighton, England, but visited many kinds of churches because he was disillusioned with the church as a whole. With a Reformed theology, his friends include the late John Stott and D. Martyn Lloyd-Jones. Terry breaks the Reformed stereotype. He and his organization, New Frontiers, have planted over one thousand churches around the world. Some years ago, Terry was filled with the Holy Spirit, and he has been influential in bringing this emphasis to the church in England and throughout the world. He is known for his teaching on the grace of God and the fullness of the Spirit. He's also known for the power of the relationships he forms with those he leads. He describes himself as "a Reformed charismatic."

Terry's influence on other pastors has a quality I find unique, powerful, warm, and wonderful. He thinks of them as part of his family, not just in lip service, but in his genuine love and commitment to them. He considers himself to be a spiritual father, and he treats his leaders like sons.

As I spent time with Terry, it dawned on me: This is what pastors are hungry for! This is why they join networks. We're all hungry for relationships—for fathers and mothers and brothers and sisters, for a family. Too often, though, our networks only accentuate the comparison and competition among us. One of the reasons is that many of our networks draw together leaders who are at similar stages of life and ministry. This demographic helps us learn from one another how to fulfill our mission, but we need more than information and ideas; we need spiritual leaders who act like fathers and mothers, who treat others like a family.

In New Frontiers, Terry is a spiritual father to about fifteen spiritual sons, and *each of them* has a number of spiritual sons. Interestingly, the relationships go far beyond theological or geographical factors. Each spiritual father has sons who are scattered around the world. It's all about the relationships, not denominations or nations.

Over the years, NorthWood has helped plant about two hundred churches. Omar Reyes is on the NorthWood staff. He also trains planters and works globally with me in many capacities. He and I began to talk about what our relationships would look like if we organized around family principles for all our churches. We analyzed the culture of our network of leaders, and we identified four common characteristics: kingdom, disciples, society, and church (KDSC). To be part of our family, we have three requirements:

> 1. They need to multiply from the start. In their first year, we want them to plant another church. They may need our help, but we want church planting to be an original value of the leaders and the congregation. The DNA of the church is established by behavior, not words in a mission statement on a page.
>
> 2. They need to care for and serve the poorest of the poor. The prophet Zechariah identified the "quartet of the vulnerable" who need our care: widows, orphans, immigrants, and the poor (Zech. 7:9–10). Jesus celebrated those who care for the hungry and thirsty, the stranger and the naked, the sick and the prisoners (Matt. 25:31–46). This commitment should be normative for church life.
>
> 3. And they need to ask God to put one of the poor or difficult places in the world on their hearts. I'll go with them there to begin or continue a ministry, and they will pour love and resources into the people they find there.

When Omar and I looked at the leaders of the two hundred churches, we didn't examine their mission statements; we examined their behavior. We identified ten men whom we were close to and who exemplified all we taught, and we brought them to meet with us. Omar and I explained that we weren't interested in creating a network. We wanted to create a family. What would it look like be a family with fathers and sons, mothers and daughters?

Omar and I weren't surprised at their response. It was the same as my response to Terry Virgo. They jumped at the opportunity, but several of them also explained, "Bob, this really doesn't change anything for us because we already consider you our spiritual father. You've just put language around it. We call you because we want to hang out with you. You're more than a source of ideas and resources for us. We belong to each other. We talk to you about our wives and our kids, our joys and our disappointments, because we trust you. And besides, you're older than us. You're about as old as our dads!"

I didn't realize it at the time, but we were creating even more than a relational capacity to love one another. We were creating a *phenomenal vehicle for exponential multiplication*. It's the way the kingdom of God is supposed to work! I love my sons, and I give them everything they need to thrive. And part of their thriving is letting them grow so they become spiritual fathers too. My sons now have sons who have sons. It's the same multiplication of love Paul encouraged when he wrote his second letter to Timothy: "You then, my child, be strengthened by the grace that is in Christ Jesus, and what you have heard from me in the presence of many witnesses entrust to faithful men who will be able to teach others also" (2 Tim. 2:1–2). There is very little dilution through these generations of our spiritual family. The implications are enormous: We don't need a huge bureaucracy or a financial infrastructure, and I don't have to spend an inordinate amount of time keeping track of everybody and everything. In developing great leaders, relationships trump institutions.

This is the cell model of a church applied to leadership and infused with family affection and commitment.

When Todd Wilson, the director of a Catalyst church-planting conference for church leaders, asked me to speak on spiritual fathers and sons, I brought my ten spiritual sons with me and asked them to sit at the front by my side. I explained to the audience that most networks begin with a vision that shapes the mission and strategy and then produces an organization to provide resources for the members. Our model is different. We begin with a vision of God's eternal purpose, but we define it as "God is building an eternal family." A vision propelled by deep, strong, authentic relationships will require an organization to provide resources, but the model is driven by love, understanding, support, and commitment. The weight of importance is always on relationships, and everything flows from them.

During the session, I asked the ten guys to talk about their involvement in the three requirements for our network. They described how they are planting churches, involved in the inner city through the domains of the community, and engaged with a full range of ministries in Pakistan, Nigeria, Vietnam, India, and other countries. They explained that all of this is setting the culture of their churches from the beginning. They're not waiting until they hit a particular size to be involved in these three parts of their mission. It all happens from day one.

The atmosphere in the meeting room was electric. Obviously, it struck a nerve—a relational nerve more than an organizational one. Immediately after the session ended, our phones lit up with texts and emails from people in the room who wanted to join our family. It's a very good problem when so many people are eager to join that we have to figure out how to adopt them and place them under a spiritual father.

All ten of these men, even if they've just started their churches, are looking for their own spiritual sons who will be committed to the same model. One of the biggest hindrances to multiplication in the American church is the perceived need for a lot of money to plant churches and be involved in cutting-edge ministry in the city domains and around the world. This model doesn't require tons of money, just tons of vision and heart.

One of the biggest differences between the global church and the American church is how we view money: we often tell the global church that money isn't necessary for them to thrive, but we act like (and worry like) it's essential here. In fact, God provides here just as he does there. Neither Rick Warren nor Bill Hybels had much money when they started their churches. They had to trust God, and faith in God isn't a bad place to live! If we keep our models of funding—and our dependence on those models—we'll *never* have a movement. Movements have to transcend money.

God provided for the early church as they were obedient to his calling, and he provides for many of our church plants as they move forward in faith. This is a clear biblical principle: God's blessings follow faithful obedience. Faith is never optional. Even if you had millions of dollars to grow your church and engage the world, you would run out of money at some point. Is God's mission over because we don't have enough funds at any point in time? No, at every point of need, we turn to God. He "has the cattle on a thousand hills," and he will provide.

The global church is often criticized for promoting a "prosperity gospel." Of course, there are excesses and wrong teaching in every land, including the United States. However, we need to understand the context of how pastors in desperately poor nations communicate hope to their people. In many cases, the people who come to church are undernourished, if not starving. They are afflicted with a myriad of diseases, many of which could be stopped by mosquito nets or inexpensive drugs, but they don't have access to these resources. Many live in areas where the rule of law has broken down and they constantly fear for their safety.

Does God care for those who are starving, poor, sick, and threatened? Is there hope for them? Is the good news of the gospel limited only to salvation? In the West, we expect God to take care of us; so do they. But our expectations and needs are very different from theirs. We typically want more affluence and personal peace— bigger houses, nicer cars, and more lavish vacations. They want the blessings of a full stomach, healthy children, and the freedom from fear that each day may be their last. That's their concept of prosperity.

Among the pastors in the Global Collaborative Community, none of them are waiting for more—size, money, or time—to reach out to make a difference. They find a way to fulfill their calling right now with few resources. But their comprehensive strategy is only part of the equation. The heart of multiplication is the relationship of spiritual fathers with their sons.

THE POWER OF STORIES

All churches have their own narratives, stories that tell who they are, how they developed, and where they're going. And all great stories are full of drama, with heroes and villains, turning points and escapes, despair and hope. The way we tell our story says volumes about our values and our faith in the sovereignty and goodness of God.

Years ago I was disillusioned with the established church and with the drive to produce megachurches. I felt pushed to look beyond the normal mission and strategy of the church. I lived with the burden of feeling like I never was measuring up, but God met me in the bottom of my deepest hole. My story, and by extension, the story of NorthWood, revolves around three revelations: the kingdom of God, the needs in the world, and the presence and power of the Holy Spirit. I love to tell people what God has done (and is still doing) in my life in these three areas.

Too often pastors focus their stories on the organization, but that seldom captures anyone's imagination. People might be impressed with the size of a building or the scope of big programs, but these seldom move their hearts. People want heroes. They want a father or mother to love them, inspire them, and propel them to greatness. They also want to be involved with a dynamic group of world changers, and they want to see themselves in that picture. The stories we tell will be far more powerful if they come from the context of life-changing relationships. But first, we need to have some of these connections.

All of us want to leave a legacy. It's one of the basic drives of human nature.[1] My legacy, the inheritance I'll leave to those who come after me, isn't the church building at NorthWood, the books I've written, or the institutions such as Glocalnet I've helped create. My legacy is people such as Kevin Cox, a pastor who today has about 180 people in his congregation and has already planted fourteen churches.

It's Scott Venable, who in three years has a church of sixty people and has planted eight churches.

It's Kevin Brown, an African American pastor who leads a church of a thousand in Philadelphia and mobilizes his members to go to the West Bank of Palestine.

Nic Burleson breaks the mold. His church, Timber Ridge, of about one thousand rednecks is in Stephenville, Texas, and he is leading his people in a ministry in Vietnam.

Sam Chako is an Indian with a multiethnic church of about a hundred in an outreach in India.

Daniel Yang is Hmong and Mike Seaman is Thai; together they have planted a multiethnic church in Toronto. Their church has outreaches to Vietnam, and they're going with me to Pakistan.

Dustin Jones was the youth pastor at NorthWood for many years and now is planting a church in our area.

Steve Bezner's situation is a little out of the box for us. He planted a church and then moved to be the pastor of a megachurch. He asked if he could be a spiritual son, and we were glad to have him. His church is committed to the same three practices, so we know the model works on a larger scale as well as a smaller one.

The oldest spiritual son is Mitch Jolly. We've worked together for almost ten years, from starting churches to working in hellholes of poverty and despair. This guy is courage, boldness, and kindness all wrapped up in one.

By the way, virtually all of my sons' and our sons' sons' churches are multiethnic, because beginning in the domains in a city or town necessarily puts us in touch with every segment of the community. Reaching domains automatically diversifies a church. If a pastor starts with a worship service in a particular neighborhood, only those people will come, but if he starts in the domains of the city—the infrastructure of government, business, medicine, the arts, communication, and the other aspects of life and culture—he'll touch every ethnic group in the community.

People might ask, "Bob, isn't all this about fathers and sons, mothers and daughters just another strategy of leadership development?" Yes, of course it's a strategy, but it's one that's birthed in and grows because of strong, committed relationships. In his covenant with the patriarchs and the nation of Israel, God often repeats his commitment: "I will be your God, and you will be my people" (e.g., Lev. 26:12). My commitment to my spiritual sons is a similar covenant: I will be your father, and you will be my sons. Covenants are based on love and loyalty, between God and his people and between spiritual fathers and sons.

My ten sons and I realize what makes us a family: the same values and goals, a trusted father, a willingness for the father to release the sons into ministry, a commitment to limitless connections with all kinds of resources to enhance their impact, working with them in their cities' domains, taking them around the world, and providing support and encouragement in all these endeavors. My connections with them are based on a family's devotion and commitment, not an organizational structure. As they experience the love and support I offer them, they follow my example.

They're finding pastors who want the same kind of relationship with a father, the same commitment and support, and they're forming their own families. They may find four or twenty, but probably the number Jesus picked (and Special Forces uses for their basic unit), twelve, is a reasonable limit.

My value to my sons, the legacy I leave with them, isn't about methodologies, because these change with cultures and times. The values I instill in them come from the wisdom, insight, and understanding I've learned over my lifetime.

In our family, love is paramount. It's the core of everything we are and everything we do. We share our hearts and we pray for each other. In this relationship, I'm vulnerable about my own struggles, fears, and needs. They'll be open with me only if I'm open with them. I ask them to pray for me as we wrestle with losing some white people in our church because we've reached out to Muslims, the poor, immigrants, and African Americans. Our church finances have taken a hit, and I ask my sons to pray that God will give me wisdom to handle the situation.

To multiply our family through generations, we emphasize the same three principles that have guided me in the past few years: the kingdom of God, meeting the needs in the domains in their communities and the world, and the filling of the Spirit to empower us to do God's will. In all of this, I don't shelter my spiritual sons from the hard choices and the threats they face when they lay it all out for Jesus. I turn them loose to follow him with all their hearts, but I'm always there to pick them up when they fall.

MODERN APOSTLES

I believe the focus on great teachers is at least one of the factors that has caused the American church to become more concentrated in megachurches, but our impact on the culture and the total number of believers aren't growing. Something's wrong, and I believe at least part of the problem is the minimized role for apostles and prophets in our country. We celebrate great preachers, we value pastoral care for the hurting, and we have evangelistic programs that involve only a fraction of the people in our churches, but the role of apostles and prophets is minimized (or nonexistent).

The DNA of the American church is very different from that of the early church, and it's very different from the DNA of the church elsewhere in the world. The vision of a bottom-up approach—of focusing on the kingdom, building multiplying disciples who are light and salt where they live and work, and planting churches from the beginning of the church's life—hasn't been part of the American church's vision, passion, or strategy. (I hope this book plays at least a small part in changing the way we do church in America.)

The role of spiritual fathers and mothers, the kind I've seen in Terry Virgo and the other global pastors—and the model I've adopted for my life and ministry—is apostolic and prophetic. To get a better grasp of the apostolic role, consider what Paul's ministry would look like today as an example of the role of spiritual fathers:

> 1. His ministry would be based out of a community
> he created, such as the one he established in Ephesus.

2. He would have a crystal-clear kingdom vision and strategy.

3. He would constantly adjust his goals and strategy based on the factors in the culture. (For example, he first went to the Jews, then the Gentiles, and then the Roman infrastructure.)

4. Change would be normative, not an exception. People who want to play it safe would feel very uncomfortable with him.

5. He would trust in the presence, purpose, and power of the Holy Spirit.

6. He would have a vision for the world, not just for his church.

7. He would spend much of his time ministering in the public domains where he and others live and work. (He knew how to relate to people far outside his tribe.)

8. He would engage people of other religions and be comfortable with them.

9. He would inflame the anger of narrow-minded religious critics.

10. He would marshal resources for the poor, sick, and needy.

11. He would exemplify a strange blend of restlessness and peace.

12. He would identify and affirm all five leadership roles in people.

13. He would equip and shepherd the leaders to multiply churches.

14. He would teach his leaders to learn on the fly. They wouldn't have to have everything figured out before they took steps of faith.

15. He would always push to reach the people on the fringes of his culture and the world. He never forgot those who had never heard of Jesus.

This list doesn't describe most pastors in America today, but it does represent many, if not most, of the hundreds of pastors I know on the far side of the globe. A pastor doesn't need a large church to live this way. Any of us can do it. Many of the leaders of small churches in America have told me this list inspires them. And a few pastors of megachurches have said they feel frustrated because the sheer size and institutional inertia of their churches inhibit them from living out this apostolic role.

When I told a friend about this list describing a modern Paul, he said, "To be honest, this sounds like a train wreck!" He asked, "What keeps someone this radical from becoming crazy, driven, and weird?" We talked about the moment when Paul told the Ephesian elders they would never see him again. They wept. They knew Paul loved them, and they loved him in return. In fact, they loved him so much that it broke their hearts to see him go. The role of an apostle isn't a power trip to dominate others. It's the role of a loving, wise, patient father who knows when to push and when to shelter his children. If love isn't the core of these relationships, they certainly can become "crazy, driven, and weird"—no more than a cult.

But apostolic leaders don't fit the profile of the typical American pastor. They don't squeeze into the neat box we've created for our leaders. They stir the pot, and they upset people by running ahead of them. Can you imagine being Paul's traveling companion and knowing he was going to incite a riot in every town and city? No wonder John Mark ran for cover. Around the world, some of the most godly and effective leaders I know are much like Paul. They're willing to take risks and shake things up. Unbelievers often adore them, but believers may feel very uncomfortable around them. I want to give these amazing leaders space to be themselves and let God use them to the max. And I also want to give American pastors room to fly. Paul was an apostle, a father to leaders of many churches. If you're a spiritual father and an apostle, you'll lead with tender love, a piercing vision, and inspiring courage—and you'll shake things up a lot. Every person in our Global Collaborative Community is much like Paul. I admire each one of them.

MY FATHERS

Let me tell you about the men who have poured themselves into my life.

My dad is a wonderful example of love and spiritual strength. He taught me to love God and his Word, the value of hard work, and the importance of welcoming everyone who wants to know and follow Jesus. To a large degree, I'm the person I am today because of him. As a little boy, I traveled with him as he preached and I went to prayer meetings with him and other pastors. My dad was the first person to take me outside the United States, to Belize in Latin America. There he became the friend of a businessman named Mr. Reyes. No one would have predicted that Mr. Reyes's son, Omar, would wind up on the NorthWood Church staff.

Leighton Ford mentored a lot of young pastors, and I was asked to be in a pilot group of twenty guys whom he would pour his life into for three years. When I was asked, I wasn't sure how they had gotten my name—or how a Presbyterian could mentor a young Baptist! He also gave us each a personal mentor. Mine was Kent Humphreys, a businessman who sold hair products to the United States military. I was so upset. Other men were being mentored by some of the finest, most respected Christian leaders in the country, and I was under a white guy who sold Afro Sheen to African American soldiers!

As I got to know Kent, I saw why Leighton had asked him to mentor me. He had started a ministry called Faith at Work, and he was one of the first leaders who saw the vocation of every believer as his or her mission from God. He gave me handles on the organizational and structural components of ministry, and he pushed me to see every believer's career as God's calling where he or she could provide value to the community and engage the world for Christ. He didn't call them domains, but he was the first person to open my eyes to this concept of God's calling.

During those years, I could already sense that I was different from a lot of other pastors I knew. Kent assured me that the difference wasn't wrong or a fatal flaw. He said, "Bob, God has given you a unique perspective and message. Don't give up on it! In fact, you're one of the few pastors I know who is releasing people to love God and people where they live and work. Don't stop!" Kent passed away a couple of years ago, far too soon, and I miss him so much. For years before his death, I picked up the phone and called him whenever I needed to, and sometimes just to talk.

Our group of twenty men gathered with Leighton about every six months. It was always an adventure. He taught me to be honest about the junk in my life. At first, we shared all the great things we were doing for God. We tried to impress one another—I'm not sure, but maybe the truth was stretched a time or two. Part of the retreat was to take inventories on our personalities and temperaments. Leighton shared the results with each of us individually. From the look on the faces of the guys coming out of the room, I knew I wasn't the only one devastated by the reports Leighton shared with us. He was brutally honest and wonderfully gracious. Somehow, my marks on those questionnaires told him things about me that I'd never shared with a soul. In our conversation, I blurted out, "I just wish I could be like you or Billy Graham!" (Leighton is Billy Graham's brother-in-law.)

He looked at me and said, "Bob, do you think we're not messed up?" He told me about some of his personal struggles. I felt so honored … and so relieved. His love and support gave me courage to be open to the truth about the darkness in my heart. I'm so grateful for his courageous honesty.

Kent Humphreys gave me encouragement, and Leighton Ford gave me hope. Another spiritual father, Bob Buford, gave me a platform. When Bob started Leadership Network, he invited me to come to a lot of their events. Most of the pastors who spoke at their gatherings had churches of thousands, but my little church was only about three hundred. Who was I to be invited? But like me, Bob is from East Texas. I guess he wanted someone around who spoke his dialect. He accepted me for who I was and believed God wanted to use me. He saw we were planting churches and developing a global network, and he gave me some money to help us make progress. It was a huge help. Having someone believe in you is a powerful tonic!

Many years later, Bob was very sick. He had been to the Mayo Clinic for treatment, but his condition wasn't improving. A number of pastors from around the world were in Dallas to meet with me, and I took them over to meet Bob. As we talked with him, we asked him if there was anything we could do for him. He said weakly, "Yes, you can pray for me." These guys know how to pray. They gathered around Bob and asked God to heal him. A few weeks later, Bob went to the Mayo Clinic again and the doctors there were amazed and confused that his condition had improved so dramatically. But Bob knew how it had happened. He often reminds me of the power of those prayers for him at a very difficult time in his life.

When I had my first meeting with top officials in Vietnam in the late '90s, my wardrobe consisted of khaki pants and Rick Warren–look-alike flowered shirts. Bob connected me to a diplomat who was a believer and was willing to teach me how to relate to other diplomats and world leaders. He took me to a men's store and bought me a very drab suit and a very plain tie. He knew I needed to look the part if I was going to meet with dignitaries and diplomats. (I shudder to think what would have happened if I'd shown up in one of those shirts!)

Bob celebrated me for living on the edge. I admire him because he's not just a successful entrepreneur. He's a brilliant thinker, a true intellectual who has a wonderful heart for God. Bob connected me with all kinds of influential people, including Bobb Biehl.

Bobb Biehl is one of the most insightful management gurus in the world. When I first met him about twenty years ago, he asked me to tell him all the things I was involved in doing. He sat back and said, "Bob, you're doing a lot of things, but they seem scattered and disconnected." He paused for a second and then asked, "Do you want to be a shrub or a tree?" Before I could answer, he told me, "You need to be a tree." (Maybe he thought I'd give the wrong answer.)

Years later when I began meeting with government officials, presidents, and kings, I felt completely out of my element. I fit better at the local Dairy Queen than the presidential palaces. I called Bobb and asked him for advice: "I have no idea how to relate to these people. I'm worried that I'm going to mess this up. Will you help me?"

He instantly said, "Let's pray." He asked God to provide someone to instruct me how to act in the presence of kings and presidents. God gave me that person, and before long, my confidence grew.

Over the years, I've had many conversations with Bobb to ask for his insights and advice. I've told him about all the things we're doing with the Global Collaborative Community, meeting ayatollahs, and visiting leaders throughout the world. In all of our conversations, I've always had his first question in the back of my mind: "Do you want to be a shrub or a tree?" A few months ago, we met again. I said, "Bobb, I want to ask you a hard question, and I want you to be brutally honest with me." He nodded. I reminded him of our talk twenty years before, and I explained, "I don't think I'm either a shrub or a tree. I couldn't say no to all the things God has put in my path to do for his kingdom. So, what am I?"

He smiled and told me, "Bob, I've grown in the past twenty years, and so have you. You're a forest. You have spiritual sons, God has used you to multiply churches, and you've engaged the leaders of nations. That's a lot of trees!"

My current spiritual father is Doug Coe, the founder of the National Prayer Breakfast. Some of the people who work with Doug get frustrated because he hasn't turned the event into a national organization. He explained, "We have enough institutions. We need to stop expecting our followers to prop up our ministries and turn them into institutions." When he said those words, I realized I felt the same way. I don't want to pour my life into a bureaucracy. I want to invest every ounce of my heart and all my resources in people, into spiritual sons, and help their dreams come true.

Jim Hylton, another spiritual father who was a pastor for over sixty years and is now a member of my church, has taught me to live in the kingdom of God and walk in the power of the Spirit. Jim didn't fit in any denomination or organizational culture; he just loves Jesus and lives for him. When I met him and heard his story, I felt as though we were twins. I don't fit in a neat box either. I didn't know how to make sense of the things God was doing in my life and the direction he was leading me, but Jim helped me see the sovereign, loving hand of God in my life. He helped me connect the dots between the kingdom of God, the mission of going to the world, and the power of the Holy Spirit. At the time, blending them all seemed confusing and difficult. Without him, I might have dismissed one of those vital components of how God has shaped my heart, my life, and my ministry.

The absence of meaningful relationships isn't just a minor inconvenience. It's a catastrophe. Sam Chand is a leadership consultant who counsels some of the most respected pastors in America and around the world. He observed:

Leaders in business, nonprofits, and churches desperately need to find someone who has no agenda except to listen without judging and love without any strings attached. The existential angst of hopelessness and despair can only be addressed in community—close relationships with at least one, preferably a few, who genuinely cares for us. Nothing less will do. Almost three out of four pastors say they regularly think of leaving the ministry,[2] many because they don't have a single close friend.[3]

He was talking about our desperate need for friends. You certainly need friends, but you need even more. You long for family connections of fathers and sons, mothers and daughters—relationships of honesty and hope, joy and tears. Ask God to open doors and lead you. Don't let pride or fear stop you. You need these people in your life.

CONSIDER THIS

See your connections with other leaders as a family instead of a corporation. Reach up to find spiritual fathers and mothers who will love you and speak into your life. Reach down to be a father or mother to a few who want God's kingdom and Spirit more than anything else in this world.

Your relationships with like-minded leaders are more important than your denomination.

As you think about your life's story, you'll probably realize you've already had many mentors and fathers and mothers in your life and you've already had an impact on a lot of young leaders to affirm them, equip them, and release them. But you could have absorbed so much more and you could have given so much more if you'd seen these relationships as familial instead of organizational.

What is your next step to identify spiritual sons or daughters?

What difference will this relationship make in their lives … and in yours?

Chapter 5

REDEFINING
SMALL GROUPS

From Optional to Foundational

In the global church, all roads lead to cells, which are small gatherings of believers. The focus is on making and multiplying disciples for the kingdom. When we hear about the incredible size of some of the churches overseas, we envision an enormous worship center with tens of thousands in a vast sea of faces. In most of these churches, however, that's not the case at all. Most of them consist of hundreds of smaller gatherings, often of five to twenty-five people, in neighborhoods. No matter how large their facilities may be, the large gathering isn't the beginning point of a person's involvement or the launchpad of growth. It's all about cells.

Eddy Leo's church began in Jakarta as a college Bible study that multiplied into many Bible studies on university campuses throughout the city. Mario Vega of Nicaragua has tens of thousands involved, but he began with a small group that multiplied. All of the churches he has planted across the globe have begun with a single cell group. Robert Lay was a Mennonite pastor whose church was stuck for years at about two hundred until he discovered the amazing growth potential of cell groups. Robert's organization, Cell Church Ministry, has trained more than twenty thousand leaders who represent the full spectrum of denominations. Many pastors, he explains, are eager to learn about the power of cells, but they want to add this concept to their existing strategy. That won't work. They have to change their mind-set, their priorities, and their strategies. The concept of cell multiplication isn't an add-on; it's a do-over. Robert is now a consultant with the pastors of some of the largest churches in the world. His strategy for these gigachurches? Think small and reproduced, scalable units.

Dion Robert was the police chief in Abidjan, Ivory Coast. After he became a Christian, he began serving in a little Baptist church. It was slowly growing, but he wasn't multiplying leaders. He discovered the strategy of cell groups, and he began to identify and equip new leaders. He now has over 250,000 in his church.

In contrast, some of the large churches in America are transplanting our nation's philosophy of church growth to some cities overseas. These congregations begin like most church plants in our country, with the emphasis on outstanding worship services, and these churches take root more easily in the parts of the world that are more familiar with Western culture.

In the West, we often argue over the model of ministry that's most effective. The leaders who plant large, exciting worship services value the ability to draw a crowd from the first day. They often dismiss a strategy that focuses on a relative handful of people who don't seem to be making much of a difference. On the other hand, the people who see cells as the answer may assume starting big is shallow and showy, a marketing angle that has little spiritual power. But the global pastors don't get into this argument. They see the value of both the small scale and the large scale. They believe in starting small, but they also realize the impact large services can have on a community. To them, it's not one or the other; it's both, and it starts and continues with cells. In Paul's letter to the believers in Ephesus, we see his description of relationships in organic cells, as well as the local congregation in the city, and the broader, universal church (cells: Eph. 4:14–17; congregation: Eph. 4:7–13; universal church: Eph. 4:1–6).

BUILDING BLOCKS

Around the world, many churches use cells and small groups as the greenhouse of personal growth and the launchpad for community impact and expansion of the kingdom. Every level of an organization needs competent, creative contributions. The roles of apostles and prophets are central in the global church, but the American church has been built on the foundation of pastors and teachers.

In Ephesians, Paul wrote, "So then you are no longer strangers and aliens, but you are fellow citizens with the saints and members of the household of God, built on the foundation of the apostles and prophets, Christ Jesus himself being the cornerstone" (Eph. 2:19–20). Some theologians teach that the role of apostles died when the Twelve passed away. I'm not concerned with the title; I'm much more interested in the function. Apostles establish the direction and the pattern of the church, and prophets speak the truth to keep the essence of the church pure.

A few years ago, Alan Hirsch wrote *The Forgotten Ways*, a book that provided the theological framework and practical application of these five functions. He wrote:

> I now believe that the idea of latent inbuilt mis-
> sional potencies is not a mere fantasy; in fact there
> are primal forces that lie latent in every Jesus com-
> munity and in every true believer. Not only does
> such a thing exist, but it is a clearly identifiable
> phenomenon that has energized history's most
> outstanding Jesus movements, perhaps the *most*
> remarkable expression of which is very much with
> us today. This extraordinary power is being recov-
> ered in certain expressions of Western Christianity,
> but not without significant challenges to, and resis-
> tance from, the current way in which we do things.[1]

Hirsch explained that when apostles and prophets are the foundation of the church, the other roles Paul identified later in this letter—pastors, teachers, and evangelists—take their God-given places in the scheme of things. Their collective role is to deepen and extend the DNA of the church, not to establish it. All of these roles are necessary for cells to thrive.

Western churches often have a few small groups, but these churches seldom are rooted and grounded in the strong connec-tions of kingdom-driven cells. In cells, everyone loves, uses gifts to

REDEFINING SMALL GROUPS   103

build others up, and serves together as they study the Bible and pray.
Everyone is part of the life of the body; everyone is fully engaged in
the spiritual community. All five roles—apostles, prophets, teachers, pastors, and evangelists—are expressed in the group. Needs are
known and joys are shared, so prayer is heartfelt. In stark contrast, in
many congregations in the West, people sit side by side but may not
even know the people around them. They watch as a few use their
gifts, and they seldom serve, if at all. It's very easy to come and go
each week as if we're going to a movie.

In many churches in the West, socialization is the primary
characteristic of small groups. Pastors sometimes say, "We're not a
church *with* small groups; we're a church *of* small groups." That's the
right language, but getting people to gather isn't the full story. For
one thing, many of these groups are birthed long after the church
is established, so the DNA of the church is primarily about the
worship hour and people volunteering to make it successful. And
many of these groups are little more than gatherings of friends, with
little, if any, vision for making a difference in the community. In
some churches, programs are offered for target groups such as men,
women, and singles, and the church also has a program for discipleship. That's the wrong metric. God hasn't commanded us to make
target-group ministries; he has commanded us to make disciples.

Having many kinds of groups isn't wrong, but it's woefully
incomplete. Groups can be far more dynamic and far more effective
than merely providing a place where people feel good about getting
together to read the Bible and pray—and eat, of course. This kind of
group is effective to encourage existing relationships and assimilate
people who are new to the church, but they aren't very effective in

producing multiplying disciples. Cells are in neighborhoods where you love, at your job where you work, at school where you learn. They are where you live your life, and they are where you have the biggest impact.

Cells aren't designed merely for fellowship. They are hothouses for discipleship, where people meet under the reign of their king and Savior, where they learn to hear and obey in an environment of grace. The leader often and always makes it clear that Christ is the head of the body and he is present by his Spirit. Cells can (and should) intentionally impart a kingdom perspective, equip people, and propel them into their domains as light and salt. People in the group are actively sharing their faith, and more are brought into the group (or new groups begin) as people in the community trust in Jesus. The role of the Holy Spirit isn't ignored or diminished. The question is often asked, "What do you hear the Spirit saying to you or to us?" The Bible is taught with a sense of wonder at God's power and grace, as well as specific applications to life situations. Hurting people are comforted, and confused people receive love and direction.

In all of this, people in the group realize they're on a mission far bigger than themselves. They live for the king, and they are bringing his kingdom to the domains where they live. When the five roles are functioning in a cell, people are mobilized to love and serve where they live and work, leaders are identified and equipped, and cells multiply.

I see this kind of cell operating in many churches around the world, but I see very few of them in America. If pastors in the West want to use groups to assimilate people and make them feel comfortable, the existing form of small groups will work just fine. But if we want to produce multiplying disciples, we need a major overhaul of our thinking and strategy.

But cells aren't the full expression of the church. In the first century, cells gathered as congregations for teaching, celebration, and the sacraments. In these times of corporate worship, their vision was refreshed and reinforced and they had access to resources they needed to be more effective where they lived and worked. In the large group, people in cells would be equipped and inspired to walk with God every day. A single cell may not make much of a dent on the entire city, but a collection of cells can be a powerful force to bring God's kingdom to every corner of the community.

ORDER AND POWER

Creating congregations is often messy. When multiple cells come together, friction inevitably occurs. People disagree about God's truth, and they have different strategies for making a difference in the city. They also may compete for authority and resources. Into this situation in the launching of the church after Pentecost, God gave deacons, elders, and bishops to provide direction and shepherd the flock of God. Church polity wasn't created to manage an existing institution; it was birthed out of the need to channel a movement of the Spirit in the lives of loving, faithful, creative people. The roles weren't established to *form* the church; they were created to *shape the impact of an expanding* church.

Some Western pastors and professors have insisted that we need polity—the right polity, of course—before God can begin to work. Instead, instituting polity only makes sense when God is working powerfully, numbers are increasing, and there's a need for structure and leadership.

Whether they realize it or not, many Christian leaders (and certainly most followers) in our country assume our heritage and culture are superior. In politics, it's called "American exceptionalism"; in the spiritual realm, we might call it "American church exceptionalism." We have many more financial and literary resources than other parts of the world and many more seminaries, gifted teachers, and almost every other benefit we can list. With all this, it's easy to feel superior. If anyone anywhere has a need, we can meet it. If anyone anywhere has a question, we can answer it.

Americans often assume accurate theology is the foundation of any movement of God. We think we need to have all of our i's dotted and our t's crossed in our theological construct before God can work. Our insistence on accuracy slows down the movement of God. It shines the light on differences, creates conflicts, and erects barriers between people who could be allies. I'm a proponent of "global theology," which contains the core beliefs of our faith and is so simple a fourth grader can explain it.

The church around the world is wonderfully diverse, brilliantly creative, and incredibly powerful. Instead of Americans being monocentric and seeing ourselves as the center of the universe, we need to become polycentric, value the wisdom and heart of leaders from other lands, and learn from our brothers and sisters overseas.

Don't get me wrong. I greatly appreciate the knowledge, resources, and generosity of church leaders in the West. For two centuries, we've sacrificed to take the gospel to the world. And our nation has helped put shattered countries back on their feet after devastating wars and natural disasters. We have much to be proud of, but no reason to be arrogant. We've opened our hearts and wallets to help people all over the world, but ironically, our power and generosity may have limited our ability to learn from those we've helped.

Some people today talk about "movements of God" in the West. I don't see any. A genuine movement is something so powerful and out of control that it's obvious God is doing it—and the media can't get enough of it. Adding a few hundred churches in the United States isn't a movement. Paulus Wiratno, a pastor in Indonesia, has trained over fifteen hundred new pastors and planted as many churches. That's a movement!

The only authentic church-planting movements in the world today are outside the West, and the vast majority of them are based on multiplying cells. Our missiologists have studied them, documented them, and published reports about them, but no one has translated the principles so they work in the Western church. If we want a church-planting movement in the United States, we'll need to humble ourselves to learn from the Chinese, the Kenyans, the Brazilians, the Indonesians, the Indians, and many others.

The global church can become our tutor to wake us up and show us what God can do through people who are open to his Spirit and plans. Years ago, Henry Blackaby suggested a novel approach to knowing and following the will of God. In *Experiencing God*, he wrote:

> We tried to find out what God already was doing
> around us. We believed that He would show us
> where He was at work, and that revelation would

be our invitation to join Him. We began praying
and watching to see what God would do next in
answer to our prayers.[2]

Those of us who have encountered the leaders of the churches
around the world have seen the incredible things God is doing among
them. He has shown us where he is at work, and he is inviting us to
join him and them. What's the next step? To join them. In many
countries of the world, we see genuine movements of God. Instead
of writing them off as anomalies or assuming we still know better, we
in the West need to find enough humility to become learners instead
of insisting we know it all.

ALL FIVE

With the basics of theology and the five roles functioning in the
group, people come with the expectation that they will hear from
God, their lives matter, and God will do amazing things in and
through them. Cells, though, aren't all exactly the same. Some are
more prophetic than others, some more evangelistic, some more
based on teaching and application, some on raising up leaders to go
into new domains in the community, and some more geared to care
for the hurting in the group. But in healthy, disciple-multiplying
groups, all of the five functions are present and identifiable.

This vision of small groups requires a radically different vision
from the pastor and the other church leaders. The concept of the
church with three expressions redefines church as we know it in
the West. The problem is that we're a nation of consumers and the

church reflects our culture. People go to church to feel better about themselves—almost like group therapy—not to celebrate the wonder of the majesty of God and be equipped to serve the king.

Consumers want to acquire comfort, thrills, and wealth. They value freedom, not submission. The idea that the God of the universe has a rightful claim on our lives is a foreign (and offensive) concept to many who sit in our churches every week. They're sure God exists to make them happy, so they have little or no desire to submit to anyone's authority—God's authority or the authority of God's representative leaders in the church. And they aren't submissive to one another in the body of Christ. They may see their friends in church as competitors for the blessings of the good life, not allies in reclaiming a lost and broken world. It's no surprise for anyone who reads Paul's letters: the key to making the church work is mutual submission under the lordship of Jesus Christ. A church doesn't have "iron sharpening iron" relationships in the worship service, and fellowship groups aren't disciple-making enterprises. Churches without dynamic, missional discipleship may have many small groups, but they probably don't have cells engaging the city. They wait for the excellence of the Sunday morning program to attract people, but they aren't equipping men and women to live for Christ all day every day in their jobs and neighborhoods.

As I've traveled around the world, I've been to churches that were birthed in this kind of discipleship. They're amazing and attractive! Our church is trying to make the change. We've seen progress, but it's hard and awkward. In his book *The Change Agent*, Lyle Schaller said change can happen in one of three ways: revolutions, but they're too bloody; reformation, but it takes too long; or innovation, which unleashes creativity.[3] This kind of change, though, starts with the shepherd, because the sheep don't have a vision for discipleship, they feel threatened by change, and they're perfectly comfortable with fellowship instead of discipleship.

American churches that adopt a strategy of disciple-making cells may not grow immediately, and in fact, they may shrink for a while. To a significant degree, the energy and resources shift from producing excellence on Sunday mornings to producing excellence in the life of cells. A lot of people who are only consumer Christians won't want to participate in the new mission. They either leave in a huff or slowly drift away. But those who catch the vision and heart of radical disciple making, even if it's only a few, will make a difference in their community, experience more spiritual life in the group than they ever imagined, and multiply themselves as their neighbors and coworkers come to Christ and become disciples. I've learned the principle that you can't let growth continue without periodic pruning—and pruning is always painful. It's not just the dead branches that need to be pruned, but the healthy ones too. Big, leafy branches may make the tree look big, but pruning makes the tree healthier and more fruitful.

As NorthWood has developed a heart for the world, our new vision is enabling us to see the world all around us. We began to reach out to the Muslims in our area. We were bold and fearless. Wouldn't that produce growth? You might think so, but we lost people. However, we've seen a tremendous benefit: it's not unusual now to see people of other religions coming to faith in Jesus at our church. Our vision also led us to a different way of selecting leaders. We didn't just welcome different ethnicities; we diversified our staff, executive staff, and elder board. Did we gain people? No, we lost people, but our church has grown culturally rich.

It's not enough for a church to have disciples who merely know and teach the Scriptures; we need to *model the kingdom*. This can't be done in isolation; it must be done in community, and it starts with the cells, which create a congregation, which then connects to the church in the rest of the world. The pursuit of numerical growth without kingdom values plunges leaders toward a credibility crash. The church that refuses to model kingdom values short-circuits long-term, sustainable growth for the sake of short-term gains.

God doesn't have two different plans for the church around the world, one for America and another for the rest of the world. He has one plan, one mission, and one strategy—with many applications. The rest of the world seems to have grasped God's heart and plan better than we have in America. It's time we all got on board.

A pastor in one of the East Asian nations led a church of about 150 for thirty years. Attendance fluctuated many times, but it never grew past that number. He became disenchanted with his ministry model, and to be honest, he was upset with himself and the Lord. Then he discovered the concept of building multiplying disciples through cells, and now his network of churches has more than two million in attendance. He spoke at a major conference for pastors in America. With very broken English, he explained, "What is the most important thing? The mission of Jesus. What did he tell people to do? Fulfill the Great Commission. In our church, we teach everybody three things. It's not complicated. First, tell people about Jesus; keep it simple. Second, put them in groups [as he described what the groups did, it felt similar to the roles in Ephesians 4]; and third, train disciples to disciple others. How do you know someone is a disciple? If they lead another cell, they're disciples."

I was on the platform with this dear pastor when he spoke that day. Dave Ferguson, the director of the conference, smiled and directed a question toward me: "Bob, break that down so we can understand it." Everybody in the room laughed. As Dave knew, it couldn't have been clearer!

Robert Lay's father had been in the SS and a ranking officer in the Nazi army. When the war was over, his family moved to Brazil to start over. As a pastor in that country, Robert has seen a magnificent movement of God. Many Brazilians have a religious background, but they haven't experienced the love and power of Jesus. They're hungry for spiritual nourishment. Robert has seen God use the power of cells to break down denominational walls. He commented, "Doctrines separate us, but the values of the kingdom unite us. We've seen Presbyterians, Baptists, Pentecostals, Catholics, and other denominations come together to live out kingdom values in the cell groups. The cells don't exist to impress people with big services or programs. They are the basic Christian community to experience the presence, power, and purpose of Christ in our midst." Today, the movement in Brazil has about fifteen hundred cell churches.

There's a big difference between "having people in small groups" and "building multiplying disciples." There's a difference between people showing up on Sunday morning to enjoy an outstanding performance and people being equipped to live for Christ every day where they live and work. There's a difference between pastors who enlist volunteers to serve in the programs at the church and group leaders who provide a hothouse of growth and mission for the people who come to their cells.

Existing churches need to take a long, hard look at their goals and structures, and many need the courage to make necessary changes. New church plants can begin with dynamic cells. Scott Venable began by creating an after-school mentoring program at an inner-city public school in Chicago. As he got to know the students and parents, he engaged in meaningful conversations about God. Some of the people he met were already believers, and some became Christians. With them, he started a cell based on the model of the five functions in this chapter. Scott and some of the believers began other programs to meet needs in different domains in their city, and more cells were formed. As the cells came together, a church was born.

Beginning a church with disciple-making DNA is exciting; changing an existing church's DNA is much more challenging, but it's possible. I know because we're doing it at NorthWood.

CONSIDER THIS

If you want to change the fundamental structure and strategy of your church, you'll have to simplify everything you're doing. The goal is no longer to produce excellent worship services to attract a lot of people who feel entertained and inspired, but to produce radical disciples of Jesus Christ.

If you have a small-group ministry, don't announce that you're going to kill it or change it. Leave it intact for now, but start your own group and instill it with the five roles Paul described in

Ephesians 4—and don't play all those roles yourself! Look for the Spirit working in the lives of others in the group. Celebrate their giftedness and let them fly. People in your congregation will notice the difference, and more people will want to taste the new wine.

As your cells grow and multiply, a new DNA will be established. Sooner or later, you'll evaluate every ministry in the church to determine if and how it is building multiplying disciples and you'll make necessary decisions.

Many pastors want their churches to be permanently and pervasively missional, but churches can't be missional without multiplying disciples. Being missional is more than an occasional event to help the poor or practice friendship evangelism with a neighbor; it's a body of people being equipped and unleashed to see the kingdom of God take root in a neighborhood, an agency, or a company.

What is God calling you to be and do?

What would it take for you to begin a new kind of group at your church, model the five functions, and see what God does with it?

Chapter 6

THE PUBLIC SQUARE

From Withdrawal to Engaging Culture

A revolution has started, but the American church isn't part of it—at least not yet.

When I was growing up, spiritual life was focused on what happened at church whenever the doors were opened: Sunday morning worship, Sunday night training, and Wednesday night prayer. From what I could tell at the time, and certainly what I've seen since I've been an adult, our church's isolated culture wasn't unique. Every church in America typically creates an enclosed society, and the only reason we band together is to protest perceived attacks on our values.

In the past, we joined other churches (even those that believed very different doctrines and had very different practices) to combat local, state, or national bills to allow the sale of alcohol, gambling, or similar propositions. We usually lost, but we felt good that we put up a good fight. Christians today are often vocal in opposition to abortion and gay rights, but actually, we don't hear much about abortion these days. It's an issue that seems to have slipped from our grasp and our minds.

It's certainly not wrong to stand up for righteousness and against sin and injustice, but if that's our only engagement with the public arena, we are easily caricatured and marginalized. The media often portrays Christians as narrow, angry, and judgmental, and too often, the portrayals are accurate. We need to do a far better job of engaging the issues of public interest. We need to engage the culture with truth, but also with respect, humility, and kindness.

On my first trip to India with Jossy Chacko, he took me to Delhi and introduced me to the leaders of the Dalits, the lowest caste in the Hindu culture. These are the people who traditionally never rise above cleaning toilets, sweeping streets, and performing only the most menial of chores. Jossy talked with them about the hopes and dreams of their people. He didn't look down on them, and he wasn't paternalistic toward them.

Later that day, Jossy took me to a meeting of leaders of the religions in India. The country has a long and volatile history of religious conflict, including the horrific battles between Muslims and Hindus when India was partitioned into two countries after World War II. Most Muslims were pushed out of their homes to live in the newly formed country of Pakistan. In the upheaval and hatred, an estimated five hundred thousand lost their lives. In our meeting, Hindu, Muslim, and Christian leaders discussed how to live together, respecting differences without killing one another. It was not an academic exercise. Religious and ethnic attacks are still common near the borders and in the cities.

As I looked around the room, I saw an evangelical Christian from Australia, Jossy, fully engaged with people of other faiths around crucial issues of public policy and culture. But our day wasn't over. When we left the meeting with the religious leaders, we went to the Parliament complex to have a meeting with lawmakers. In this discussion, he represented the interests of the Dalits, the Hindus, and the Muslims, as well as the Christians in the country. Jossy was positioned as a respected, informed dealmaker, to a large degree because he is also a peacemaker. His influence was earned by his business expertise. The leaders in the country listened because he put thousands of Indians to work. Everything he accomplished in his cultural engagement was based on the relationships he and his family had earned through their business success.

Jossy, as I've pointed out, has identified and trained thousands of church planters in India, and virtually all of these began their work by serving in one of the domains of their communities. When they set up sewing centers, they provide jobs; when they establish schools, they educate children who may not have had the chance to learn to read and write; when they create markets, they give farmers the opportunity to make a living. And as they serve the community with integrity, respect, excellence, and kindness, people are more open to discussions about Jesus Christ. In India, the red tape to open any business can crush a person's motivation,[1] but when government officials hear Jossy's name, they more readily open the doors for his army of visionary servants.

ALLY OR ANTAGONIST

As I've traveled around the world, I've seen a bipolar Christian worldview: a few such as Jossy and the other pastors in the Global

Collaborative Community are fully engaged in the public square, but others, including many church leaders in America, have embraced a combative stance; they see modern culture as a threat, and they fight against it. This perspective effectively creates an "us against them" mentality in their followers, and it crushes any chance for meaningful engagement.

In countries where Christians are in the minority, believers are forced to be more respectful of other religions and more creative in earning a hearing for their views. In many countries, they have to lobby for religious freedoms to live and worship. To earn those rights, they have to prove they are contributors to the public good, not just antagonists who demand their rights and then pout when they don't get their way.

A commitment to engage in the public square is an even higher level than participation in communal domains. In the public square, we build relationships with leaders in government, science, medicine, and other religions. These relationships then pave the way for our people to open clinics, schools, shops, and markets.

When we become friends with leaders in these countries, provinces, and cities, they lower their defenses and they want to hear our message. Today, people around the world listen to my messages every Sunday, not because I'm as gifted as Tim Keller or Matt Chandler, but because civic leaders have told people they trust me … and some of them even like me. I've learned that our highest value as pastors isn't our preaching; it's our involvement in the public square to engage leaders in the religious, political, and business worlds; build relationships; earn credibility; and serve the community—and through all this, create opportunities for people to hear the gospel of grace. By serving in the public square, we earn a hearing and we have a voice. We want a voice because we're preachers, but the culture gives us a hearing when they see us serving with kindness, tenacity, and faithfulness.

Unfortunately, the last hundred years have seen a withdrawal from the public arena on the part of evangelicals. Early in the last century, our leaders recoiled from the "social gospel" that undermined the authority of Scripture and turned its attention to care for the poor, the sick, and the downtrodden. The Fundamentalists wrote and spoke to retake the high ground of biblical inerrancy, but in their fight with the liberals, they invested most of their energy in theological debates, leaving the work in hospitals, schools, and poor parts of communities to the liberals. The debates were largely won and lost in the early twentieth century, but the effects have lingered for decades. Evangelicals are still largely reactionary, defending the authority of Scripture and seeing social change as a threat. Thankfully, we see genuine vision and creative involvement in the social arena by some churches, but we have a long way to go to build real credibility.[2]

Today, I receive invitations to speak to many different government, religious, and civic groups around the world, not because I'm the most gifted speaker, but because our church has invested heart, time, and tangible resources in helping people in those communities. Christian businesspeople in our church, both men and women, mentor those who want to start businesses in an East Asian country; our people have written curricula for students with special needs in countries that didn't have this kind of educational resource; we dig wells for communities that have had to walk for hours to find drinkable water; we teach skills so people can find good-paying jobs and earn a living for their families; we've helped farmers buy water buffaloes so they can be more productive; and the list goes on and on. To uncover these opportunities, we have to observe, ask plenty of questions, and listen long and hard so we genuinely grasp the need and the right way to step in to meet the need. If we're perceived as arrogant imperialists or colonialists, we lose the opportunity to make a difference.

The first goal of a missionary isn't to start a church. The first and foremost task of missionaries is to serve in the community so that people who come to Christ realize their jobs and community relationships are their God-given environments where they can serve him. The job itself is a calling from God, and those who work are serving their communities and building credibility. Our focus on the domains in any community, however, often happens more effectively if Christian leaders first build connections with religious and civic leaders.

I've learned that there are only two reasons anyone is able to stand before a king. First, we may stand in his presence because someone introduces us; and second, we are invited to the throne because the king has learned that we've effectively served him and his people. I've stood before presidents, kings, imams, sultans, and prime ministers for both of these reasons. I'm grateful for the introductions, but I'm thrilled when a nation's leader thanks me for contributing to the success of his people.

Along with ten other Americans, I was invited to meet with the general secretary of Vietnam, the first visit of someone in that position to the United States. His schedule included a meeting with President Obama in the morning and us in the afternoon. I was there because we've worked in Vietnam for twenty years, in over eighty projects, mobilizing twenty-five hundred people and investing millions of dollars. Later that evening, I spoke at an iftar (an evening meal breaking the daily fast during Ramadan) at the ADAMS Center Mosque near Dulles Airport outside Washington, DC. Why? Because the imam and I have been working together to protect religious minorities in Pakistan and around the world. Engagement opens the doors.

UNCOMMON ETIQUETTE

To engage leaders in the public arena, we need to learn the fine art of etiquette. Some Christian leaders in America have built their reputations by being abrasive, antagonistic, and furious. At this point in our history, they can get away with this stance because we're still in the majority, but a day may be coming when we will no longer have that option. But even today, delighting in condemnation is a very poor strategy for advancing the kingdom. It creates enemies and raises their defenses instead of building bridges that can lead to more opportunities for the gospel. We don't have to agree with the leaders of government, medicine, media, education, and science, but we need to at least be civil in our disagreements.

Let me suggest a few principles of etiquette:

Respect Authority

Instead of immediately identifying the differences—"a gay mayor," "a liberal senator," "a flip-flopping candidate"—realize God has put every person in authority in his or her place (Rom. 13:1–2). Walk through the front door of honor and respect, not the back door of blame and innuendo.

Practice Civility

Instead of viewing the person in authority as an enemy or a target of necessarily manipulative techniques to get your way, treat the person the way you'd treat a friend. That's what civility is. Don't be hateful; be nice. Smile. And watch what you say about the person to your allies. Sometimes the statements we make in private find the ears of those we criticize. Solomon's words remind us, "Even in your thoughts, do not curse the king, nor in your bedroom curse the rich, for a bird of the air will carry your voice, or some winged creature tell the matter" (Eccl. 10:20).

Be a Good Citizen

Instead of finding fault, look for ways to support people of different races, religions, and classes. The Puritans tried very hard to establish God's kingdom on earth when they landed in the New World, but they eventually realized God works through common grace, the generosity of God to all people. Jesus said, "For he makes his sun rise on the evil and on the good, and sends rain on the just and on the unjust" (Matt. 5:45). Celebrate every person who contributes to the good of the community. Be known as a person with a grateful heart.

Understand Protocol

We may shake our heads when we watch period movies about the extravagantly choreographed ways subjects approached the monarchs of England or France in earlier centuries, and we may still be amazed at the instructions given to those who are introduced to mayors and governors. However, it's not all ridiculous. The protocol of relating to leaders displays honor for the position.

I've learned to be quiet when I meet with leaders. Sometimes I take people with me to meet with presidents and kings. These people know me as a loud, talkative guy, and they're stunned that I'm silent in these meetings. It would be totally inappropriate for me to treat one of these leaders like a buddy at a ball game. Listening far more than I speak shows honor for them. Protocol means knowing when to open your mouth and when to shut it.

When I take young pastors and leaders to a mayor's office, to the White House, or to meet other leaders, I give them a tutorial: here's how you should dress, how you walk in, how you greet the leader, where you sit, what to say when a question is asked, and on and on. These things matter.

Before King Abdullah of Saudi Arabia died, Prince Turki al-Faisal invited my wife and me to Riyadh. The prince scheduled me to meet with Faisal bin Abdulrahman bin Muaammar, secretary-general of the King Abdullah bin Abdulaziz International Center for Interreligious and Intercultural Dialogue in Vienna, Austria. He asked me to speak at a conference and then attend a banquet at a hotel in Vienna. When I arrived, jet lag was killing me. I wanted to just go to bed. I had already missed one meeting, but when I got to my room, I found a note reminding me of two remaining meetings. The note urged me to come. I really didn't want to go because I was exhausted, but I took a shower, put on a suit, and went to the meeting.

When I arrived, the meeting had already begun, so instead of opening the door, I stood outside until it was over. When it finished, the organizer and a couple of the princes of Saudi Arabia walked down the hall toward me. I tried to fade into the wallpaper, but I'm too big for that. I then tried to look as inconspicuous as possible. My friend saw me and shouted, "Bob, it's so good to see you! I want you to meet the prince!" He introduced me to a number of people in the royal family. After they entered a room for the banquet and sat down, I followed and sat at a table in the back of the room. A few minutes later, my friend found me in the back of the room and asked me to come to sit at the table with the family. Before I left the table, a reporter turned to me and asked, "People here know you. Who are you?"

I said, "I'm Bob Roberts."

He asked, "What do you do?"

"I'm a minister," I told him.

He looked puzzled and said, "Which department of government?"

"Oh," I explained, "not that kind of minister. I'm a pastor."

He looked shocked. "How did a pastor from America become friends with the royal family of Saudi Arabia?"

"It's a long story," I told him as I got up to walk to the front.

When I sat down, my friend asked me to tell the princes stories about my relationships with Islamic leaders in other countries in the Middle East. If I'd assumed I would sit at the head table when I came down for the banquet, I may have been deeply embarrassed. But by taking the lowest place, as Jesus suggested, I was given a place of honor. That's how protocol worked in the parable of the kingdom, and it's how it still works in meetings with leaders today.

Build Credibility

We don't have instant credibility with anyone, especially leaders. We can establish our credibility over time by demonstrating character and results. As the saying goes, "Under-promise and over-deliver." Don't make bold promises and try to make a dramatic beginning with a big program. It's far better to start small and show results over time. I encourage our leaders to find some way to serve the community in a consistent, reproducible way over a long period. Flashes in the pan, even if they're successful, don't make as much of an impression on civic and religious leaders.

Keep a Calm Spirit

Be prepared and know what you want to say when leaders ask hard questions. Some of them want to take the measure of your confidence and character, and they ask difficult questions to see how you'll respond. Don't try to impress them with vast knowledge. Instead, give simple, clear answers. If you don't know, don't be thrown for a loop and don't be defensive. Say, "That's a good question, but I don't know the answer," and make a commitment to find the answer and give a report later.

Integrate All of Your Life

Instead of "living in two worlds," the sacred and the secular, develop a worldview of common grace like the Puritans. Every vocation has value, to God and to the community. Every moment is sacred, whether we're spending time with family, spending time with people of other faiths, serving in our domains, or worshipping in church. When Christians fail to integrate their lives into a cohesive whole, they often pick sides—the good people and the bad people, the insiders and the outsiders—which sets them up against the people God wants them to touch with his love, kindness, forgiveness, wisdom, and strength.

Our agenda isn't to get the message of the church into the public arena. When we elbow our way and insist on being heard, we erect more walls than bridges. Christians who truly integrate their faith in their jobs and neighborhoods don't see unbelievers as projects or targets; they see them as friends. Look at the life of Jesus, "a friend of sinners." Too often, Christians act more like Pharisees than like Jesus, creating more enemies than friends and losing any chance of having a positive impact on the people around us.

If secular people know we love them for who they are, they won't be on guard when we open our mouths. In fact, they'll want our input and they'll ask us to speak at their events.

Is there ever a time to speak out against public policies that promote sin and harm people? Certainly, but we will be heard only if we've already built friendships with those who are listening, and we won't be heard if our voices are shrill, demanding, and condemning.

If we can learn and apply these principles, we will find doors opening to us to talk about Jesus in places we never dreamed possible. I've been asked to speak at mosques in America and at Islamic conferences around the world. I've been invited to speak at synagogues and at diplomatic functions. When people find out that Bob Roberts—Bob Roberts, for crying out loud!—has been asked to come to speak at these places, they wonder two things: Why in the world would these people ask me to come? And why in the world would I go, even if I were invited? I can answer the first question only by saying that I've tried my best to treat people with respect. In response to the second question, I point to the work of the apostle Paul over nineteen centuries ago. He entered the public square to meet with leaders of synagogues, Roman rulers, philosophers, civic officials, military officers, and business leaders. I'm only trying to follow his lead. His proclamation of the gospel often happened at religious and civic events.

Most pastors and Christian leaders in America aren't fully present to build relationships with leaders in the public square, and our people aren't fully engaged in the domains in our communities. Building relationships with leaders opens doors to serve in the domains, and serving in the domains then builds more credibility with civic and religious leaders. Most of us aren't doing a good job of following Paul's example.

I received an invitation to speak at the Islamic Association of North America where forty thousand Muslims gather annually. When I met with the conference directors before I spoke, one of them said to me, "Bob, Muslims and Christians have many points on which we agree." He was trying to say our differences aren't that great. I don't agree, but I want to disagree in a way that shows respect.

I responded, "Yes, but the test of a mature faith is to love each other even though we disagree. You believe Jesus was a prophet. We believe he was God in the flesh. You don't believe he was raised from the dead; we do. Our orthodoxy is your heresy, and your orthodoxy is our heresy. If we love and respect each other, we don't need to hide those things." I wanted to go further, so I paused and then said, "Hey, I want to baptize every one of you." They all laughed. I then said, "And many of you want me to become a Muslim. I'm honored by that. I love you so much that I want you to be with me for all eternity, and you care about me in the same way. This is how friends are: they want the other to love the same things they love and enjoy the same things they enjoy."

I don't break out a gospel booklet or any other presentation. It's relational, very relational. And I use the same kind of communication style with the government officials, business leaders, and the top level of any religion wherever I travel in the world. Some might say, "Well, you're not as clear as you might be." I disagree. The message of the divinity of Christ, his saving work on the cross, and the hope of the resurrection is crystal clear. I just don't offend them by making it sound canned, demanding, and impersonal.

Some insensitive pastors make dramatic, poisonous pronouncements about the prophet Mohammed. They may stand up and tell their crowd, "Mohammed was a pedophile!" The crowd loves it because they can then feel superior to all Muslims; but what does this statement (and others like it) do for our ability to connect and share the gospel of grace with Muslims in our country and around the world? Jesus didn't trash other religions. To the woman at the well, he explained that she was seeking truth and he was the ultimate truth: "I'm the one you're looking for" (see John 4:19–26). Paul made the same point in Athens: "You're worshipping unknown gods, but I have the privilege of revealing him to you" (see Acts 17:22–31).

I've never seen anyone come to faith in Christ because someone trashed their religion so badly it convinced them to repent. The kindness of God—and of God's people—leads people to repentance, not harsh condemnation, fear, and fury. On the other hand, I've seen many people trust in Christ because believers have lovingly communicated the truth to them, just as Jesus spoke to the woman and Paul talked to the leaders on Mars Hill. When people realize we love them, something very odd happens: people we never imagined would be interested in Jesus—government officials, media stars, business leaders, and even some top leaders in other religions—become curious about Christ. That's not just wishful thinking; I've seen it with my own eyes.

Why did people flock to Jesus during his earthly ministry, and why did so many believe the gospel in the first days after Pentecost? Jesus amazed people with his truth and grace, and the early church demonstrated the same attractive combination. The Jews weren't looking for a different religion, and the Samaritans and Romans were sure they were right too—until the love of God, expressed by believers, captured their hearts. The gospel isn't a competing religious system to earn God's acceptance. It's a totally different way of relating to God, based on Jesus's sacrifice for us instead of our efforts to prove we're worthy of him.

The gospel offers God's limitless forgiveness instead of the option of spending a lifetime trying to feel bad enough long enough to compensate for every sin—and knowing it's never enough. The gospel tells us that Jesus is our treasure and we are his. And the gospel creates a new kind of family, of adopted sons and daughters who experience the Father's love, wisdom, and strength. Nothing like that has ever been communicated to most people of the world, and many of them are hungry for it!

To function in the public square, we need a bigger gospel. In America, we talk a lot about Jesus, but the subtext is often "do more for Jesus" or "be more passionate about Jesus" to prove you're acceptable to him. We may assure people that the gospel of grace gets them into heaven, but after they're saved, we too often communicate that they need to work hard to earn God's acceptance. That's not the message of the New Testament! We never leave the gospel behind. It's our original source of forgiveness and assurance, and it's our continuing source of motivation to live and love the way Jesus lived and loves us now.

Paul put it succinctly: "For the love of Christ controls us, because we have concluded this: that one has died for all, therefore all have died; and he died for all, that those who live might no longer live for themselves but for him who for their sake died and was raised" (2 Cor. 5:14–15). And to the Ephesians, he explained the connection between the saving grace of Jesus and our present motivation: "Therefore be imitators of God, as beloved children. And walk in love, as Christ loved us and gave himself up for us, a fragrant offering and sacrifice to God" (Eph. 5:1–2). These, of course, are only two pearls from a treasure chest of passages that continually point us to the grace of Christ to melt our hearts and mold us a little more into his likeness.

Paul knew how to speak in the public square. He could relate on their level without being defensive or condemning. He was bold when he was under attack, but he was loving and gracious in sharing the message of Christ. He was so persuasive that a city official protected him in Ephesus (see Acts 19:35–40), and King Agrippa was so moved that he replied, "In a short time would you persuade me to be a Christian?" Paul answered him, "Whether short or long, I would to God that not only you but also all who hear me this day might become such as I am—except for these chains" (Acts 26:27–29). Agrippa didn't feel attacked by Paul, even though he was the ruler of the oppressive occupying force of Rome. Instead, the king felt moved by the love of Paul and his message about Jesus.

If we genuinely want to reach the world, we have to take the gospel out of the confines of the church and impart it to the public square.

Christian leaders need to engage the leaders of the public domains, and believers need to love people in those same domains where they live and work. In America, most of us—pastors and church members—are either irrelevant or demanding. Our people keep their faith private, so we have no impact on the people in our neighborhoods and at work, or we screech and condemn the "evil society" for challenging our values. Neither of these tactics has a positive influence.

Paul had a better way. He wrote the Christians in Colossae:

> Continue steadfastly in prayer, being watchful in it with thanksgiving. At the same time, pray also for us, that God may open to us a door for the word, to declare the mystery of Christ, on account of which I am in prison—that I may make it clear, which is how I ought to speak.
>
> Walk in wisdom toward outsiders, making the best use of the time. Let your speech always be gracious, seasoned with salt, so that you may know how you ought to answer each person. (Col. 4:2–6)

Paul asked for prayer that God would give him open doors to share the gospel in his public domain: at the time, the prison. And he gave the Christians in Colossae instructions about engaging their domains with gracious attitudes and gracious words.

When riots broke out in Baltimore in the spring of 2015 over the death of a young black man who had been apprehended by police, some white Christians wanted to come to the city to offer their help. Wise black leaders gave them this advice: "If you come, don't trash President Obama. We respect him. If you condemn him, you'll spread more strife instead of the love of God. You'll do more harm than good." Christian leaders and their people can be of great help in any community, but only if they engage with humility, sensitivity, and respect.

If Christian leaders learn how to engage officials in the public square, no nation is closed to our message or to us. Some of my colleagues and I have opened doors in countries that have been the most antagonistic to the church. In every nation, we've seen that religion isn't attractive to others, but love, selfless service, and a little humor open many doors.

In all of our communication, we can't afford to be two faced. We need to say the same thing privately as we do publicly. If our love for leaders is only a mask and we actually despise them, they'll sense it. But if our love for them is real, and we have nothing to hide, they'll sense that too.

CONSIDER THIS

One of my spiritual sons, Kevin Cox, began after-school programs for kids in his community near Dallas. Parents and children were so impressed, they told the principal about the work he and his team were doing. The principal watched them for a long time, and at one point, he called Kevin in for a talk. He explained that Kevin had done such a good job that he wanted him to run for the school board.

Kevin's love and excellent service won the hearts of kids and parents, then the teachers, and finally the principal. He earned relational capital he could invest in reaching leaders in his community. Doors opened in the public square.

How are you and your people building credibility in the domains of your community? When you're making a difference, you'll know it. Leaders in the community will want to meet with you.

What are the messages you and your church are communicating about gays, Muslims, immigrants, the poor, and others who might be considered outcasts or undesirables? Which messages are offensive and divisive, and which messages are gracious and inviting?

How big is your gospel? What would it look like for your love to extend to the leaders of government, business, education, and the other domains?

Make a list of these people, and begin meeting with them.

Chapter 7

ENGAGING OTHER FAITHS

From Afraid and Isolated to Loving and Involved

In the '90s, we took a number of professionals from NorthWood to Vietnam to let them share their expertise in corresponding domains in that country. It was our first foray into the much bigger world. I had to figure out how to relate to the officials of a communist government with tact and diplomacy, and in the communities of Vietnam, we had to discover how to relate to many people who follow the traditional faiths in that country: Buddhism, ancestor worship, and atheism, their relatively new *un*belief system.

For many years, I completely ignored political and religious leaders. Then I began to see them as doors—sometimes open, sometimes closed—to get into the domains of their nations; but until I began meeting with the pastors in the Global Collaborative Community, I didn't try to reach these leaders. I discovered that the religious leaders of other faiths aren't necessarily enemies. These leaders can be friends and allies, and in fact, some of them become brothers and sisters. Relating to leaders of these religions requires a blend of compassion, wisdom, diplomacy, and courage.

After a tsunami devastated much of the Indonesian shoreline of the Indian Ocean on December 26, 2004, I flew to Aceh, the province closest to the epicenter of the quake, to see if our church could help. I met Eddy Leo and the leaders from Abba Love Church, and I realized they had a bigger vision than merely offering a few resources to meet the immediate needs. Much of the region is Muslim, and many mosques had been destroyed. The churches of the small Christian community had also been washed away. The leaders of Abba Love Church realized the Christians desperately needed help, but they also understood they could have a far wider impact on the community if they had a more inclusive strategy. They raised money for construction projects, not just to rebuild churches, but to rebuild many mosques as well. As a result, when the Christians began rebuilding the mosques, the Muslims permitted the Christians to rebuild their church, build it larger, and even construct some new churches because of the growth of Christianity in the area. It was an astounding demonstration of solidarity and cooperation.

In America, many Christians would claim the leaders of Abba Love Church had compromised their values (and sanity) by pouring resources into mosques, but this generous act helped build trust in a country where religious hatred and warfare had taken thousands of lives in recent years. When Americans see differences in religions, we often visualize a war of cultures—and we have to win—and at times we have demonized those who are different from us. Of course, the images of ISIS terrorists beheading individuals and murdering hundreds at a time don't exactly lower walls and inspire trust. They are horrific and evil to the furthest degree; but I believe we use far too broad a brush and paint too many people as enemies.

When we despise and distrust reasonable leaders and ordinary people of other faiths, we create enemies instead of friends. We already have enough enemies; we don't need any more. Recently, Imam Mohamed Magid of the ADAMS Center Mosque near Washington, DC, collected money from people in his mosque to help rebuild a Pakistani church that had been burned down by extremists. They raised tens of thousands of dollars. (I was sad there was no news coverage of his leadership and their generosity.)

Instead of hiding behind walls or running away from Muslims in Mombasa, Joseph Maisha initiated conversations with Islamic leaders and neighbors. As he got to know them, he discovered their needs and he found ways to serve them. He opened an orphanage and a school, but not just for Christian children. He welcomed Muslim kids and honored their faith by asking an imam to teach the Koran to Muslim children. Joseph gave to the school scholarships for children of Muslims, a gesture that built a lot of credibility with Muslim leaders in the city. The imams were so impressed with Joseph and his work that they named him chairman of the board to develop education. At that point, he was able to build relationships from the top to the bottom of the Muslim community. Many Muslims have come to his church to ask for prayer. Even if they haven't trusted Christ, Joseph prays for them and provides resources to meet their needs. Because of his bold love, gracious spirit, and tangible service, over eleven hundred Muslims have come to Christ. And now, these people are living examples of the love of Christ among their own people.

When doctors come from France or America to provide services for a week or a month, Joseph's church welcomes Muslims as well as Christians to receive medical care. Again, serving people with specific services tears down walls and builds bridges. As he reflected on the hesitancy of many Christians to reach out to people of other religions, Joseph raised some good points:

> I don't know why some of my fellow Christians find it so impossible to relate to people of other faiths. We live in the same communities, use the same services, drive on the same streets, shop at the same stores, and drink the same water. A Buddhist who lives near me is my neighbor. A Muslim who lives around the corner is my neighbor. An atheist or an animist who lives down the street is my neighbor. We can be friends. We *must* be friends if we want to have an influence on them for Jesus Christ. The Muslims in our community know that I don't hate them, and I don't force them to believe as I do. They know what I believe, but they also know I love them. God has given me such a good relationship with some of the Muslim leaders that we kid each other. I say, "Why don't you come to my church so I can baptize you?" And he says, "Come to my mosque and I'll turn you into an imam." We laugh together. It shows that we're very comfortable with each other, and we can easily discuss religion, the needs in our community, and our plans to meet

those needs—together, not as enemies. People who
hate one another can't build the kingdom of God. It
can only be achieved when we humbly serve people
and trust God to convert them.

Working with religious leaders also has practical benefits. When
Islamic terrorists crossed the border from Somalia and threatened
Christians in Kenya, the Muslim leaders in Mombasa provided pro-
tection for Joseph and the people in his church.

THE CHALLENGE FOR AMERICANS

Only a generation ago, most Christians in America seldom had contact with people of other faiths. To many of them, the battle lines
were drawn between Baptists and Methodists, between Presbyterians
and Pentecostals, and between Catholics and Protestants. In recent
years, however, our world has changed. Most communities have far
more diversity. Immigrants and refugees have come in unprecedented
numbers. For instance, a small town in Georgia that formerly had
only whites and African Americans now is 27 percent Hispanic.[1]
Like virtually all cities in America, Chicago has seen a flood of immigrants in the past decades. Civil wars and ethnic strife in Africa have
caused refugees to flee to the city from Sierra Leone, Uganda, the
Congo, Ethiopia, Somalia, Cameroon, Nigeria, Angola, and Sudan.
From the Middle East, people have fled war and oppression from
Iraq, Lebanon, Palestine, and Syria. And from Central America and
South America, people from many countries have sought safety from
repressive regimes, wars, and poverty.[2]

These two examples represent virtually every town and city across our country. The people who have moved into our communities sometimes don't speak English; they don't dress like we dress or eat the same foods we eat. There are, then, natural barriers between them and us. Instead of getting to know them, it's easy to stand back and observe, or be suspicious, or resent them because our government offers them social services.

Our great country is founded on the concept of pluralism, but too many Christians despise the idea of inclusion. That's a tragedy. We're missing one of the greatest opportunities imaginable to fulfill the Great Commission! All of these communities of other faiths, here and abroad, have leaders. As I mentioned, I used to think God had given me access to these leaders as open doors to care for and reach their people. That's true, but there's more: God gave me access to them because he loves each one of them and wants them to know him. They aren't just channels for us to share the love of God; God wants *them* to experience his love, forgiveness, power, and hope.

When we say the word "evangelical" in America, we mean almost exclusively white conservative Republicans. That's too narrow and restrictive for the kingdom of God! If people from other cultures, here or abroad, only hear us and see images of committed, born-again Christians angrily denouncing them and blocking access to social services, what will they conclude about our God?

To change the reputation of American evangelicals, we can't launch a slick media campaign and expect it to work. We have to get to know people of other faiths and other nations, and they have to be convinced that we love them. And beyond the ordinary people of those lands and religions, we need to build friendships with their leaders.

In our church-planting ministry, we teach our spiritual sons and daughters to talk about "multi-faith" instead of "interfaith." The idea of "interfaith" is that all religions are equally true and valuable and all roads lead to heaven. We don't believe that, and neither do the leaders of most religions. Instead, we can respect the differences without condescension or condemnation.

We encourage our leaders to develop a script to talk with religious leaders about Christ. We tell them, "Be as clear and as kind as you can be." Developing a clear and simple message takes work, but it's absolutely necessary.

We also tell our leaders to follow the right order of involvement: hand, then heart, and then head. Too often, Christians begin by trying to convince other leaders that our truth is better than their truth. We almost never get anywhere with this approach. We'll build far more trust if we first serve consistently and graciously. When we sweat together serving with people of other faiths, we prove we care and we get to know them as human beings. Only then can we share our hearts—our hopes and fears, our joys and struggles. And only then, when we understand each other, will the other person be open to a gracious, nonthreatening, relaxed conversation about our faith. In the context of respect and love, we won't demand compliance with our beliefs. We'll share with each other as trusted friends.

When I train young pastors, I often take them to a mosque or synagogue for our lessons. Sometimes an imam or a rabbi is in the room as we talk. I invite the imam or rabbi to join the conversation, and I model having a respectful conversation with a leader of another religion. Quite often, the other leader gives a dissenting view, and I welcome the differing opinion. It gives me an opportunity to clarify my point without being defensive or demeaning. We still get our lesson across, but the added layer of discussing theology or strategy in the presence of a leader of another faith adds a lot of spice to the conversation. (You should try it!)

By the way, I grew up believing Catholics were the "other religion." As I've traveled around the world, I've met some Catholics who genuinely love Jesus and experience his grace and power. We still don't agree on a number of issues, such as Mary or the sacraments or purgatory, but with at least some, we share a common bond in the fullness of the sacrifice of Jesus to pay for our sins. Some of these grace-believing Catholics, leaders and followers, pay a price to follow Jesus in their churches. I have great respect for them. (Recently, Father James Channan of Pakistan released his book, *Path of Love*, that describes the interfaith work between Catholics and Muslims in Pakistan. At a meeting in the Tillman Chapel of the United Nations, Father Channan received a peace award and I was privileged to give a speech to honor him.)

Of course, respect works both ways. If I try to have a conversation with a religious leader who is suspicious or angry, I can try to build bridges, but some of them are just as narrow and resentful as some American evangelical leaders. I have to shake the dust off my feet and move on.

I encourage my spiritual sons, "Make friends with the imam, the priest, and the rabbi in your community. Take them out to eat at the restaurant of their choosing, and ask them to order for you. Invite them to spend time in your home. Ask about their families, their backgrounds, and their hobbies. Treat them like friends, and they might just become your friends."

As we learn to minister in the public square, we meet leaders of every political and religious persuasion. As we interact with them, we learn to talk more simply and clearly about Jesus in a pluralistic world.

Americans say we believe in religious freedom, but too often, we really only care about religious freedom for Christians. We seldom defend the rights of minority religions to practice their faith, and we're deeply offended when their practices clash with ours. If we speak out for their rights, we'll probably shock them and our own people, but we'll build a connection that may have very positive and lasting results.

The clash of cultures can become very personal. One of the problems in the Christian subculture today is that we're overly protective of our children. We send our kids to Christian schools so they won't be exposed to drugs, sex, and other religions. But we make two mistakes: first, we believe kids in the Christian schools don't do drugs, don't have sex, and always believe the Bible; and second, we fail to teach our kids how to handle temptation and relate to people of other faiths. When our teenagers go off to college, we are shocked that our kids aren't prepared to handle temptation and diversity. If our strategy for our kids is keeping them away from unbelieving kids, we're sunk. We'll raise immature young people who don't have enough wisdom and savvy to relate to real people in the real world. It seems that we assume our faith is too fragile and vulnerable to let it be tested, or we're too lazy or distracted to impart a strong faith to our children.

PUSHBACK

When we reach out to build relationships with leaders of other faiths, the narrow and rigid Christians accuse us of watering down our convictions. To them, any difference is black or white, a battle against good and evil, and they're sure they're always on the side of good.

How far are we willing to go? It's one thing to eat at an ethnic restaurant. People don't mind that. They may not care if we're nice to our neighbors down the street who are from a distant land, and they're willing to send money or other resources to an agency to care for "those people." But many Christians are up in arms when they hear their pastor has become friends with an imam, a rabbi, a monk, or a priest. They whisper behind our backs, stand up in meetings to question our motives, and accuse us of caving in to the enemy.

But that's exactly the point: Jesus didn't see Samaritans and Romans as enemies. He saw them as people who desperately needed the love of God, and he died for them. Even Pilate wanted to set Jesus free. The fiercest opposition came from the leaders of his own faith, the self-righteous Pharisees and the Sadducees who collaborated with the Romans. For many Christians, it's much easier to be judgmental and distant than to love people of other faiths. Jesus took initiative to meet the Samaritan woman at the well, but James and John wanted to call down fire to consume Samaritans!

The pushback you'll experience probably won't be from the religious leaders you're trying to befriend. It will come from your own staff, board, and friends who are pastors—from your own tribe. One of the accusations we may hear is that we've lost our focus, we've compromised our values, or we're wasting too much time on people who aren't open to the gospel. The answer to the first two is that we're doing exactly what God has called us to do. The answer to the third objection is more complex. Let me explain.

Too often, our evangelism is episodic: we share the message and expect people immediately to pray a prayer. A few decades ago when the American culture had a strong Christian ethic and subtext, many people responded to the first exposure to Evangelism Explosion, the Four Spiritual Laws, or Steps to Faith in God. But today throughout the culture and especially in relating to people of other faiths, we need a very different set of assumptions. We have to do much more plowing, sowing, and watering before people believe the gospel, so we must be far more patient, gracious, persistent, and kind in the long process of loving them into the kingdom.

If we share the gospel with people and offer to be their friends, what happens when they're slow to respond? Do we no longer treat them as friends? One of the most astounding things about the life of Jesus is how comfortable outcasts felt around him. They didn't feel pressured to perform, to repent, or to follow religious rules to be accepted. They knew he loved them, with no strings attached.

When we experience opposition from our own people, we need to be as gracious and as patient—and as direct—as Jesus was with the Pharisees. Jesus told them the truth, correcting their misconceptions about the purposes of God and the breadth of God's love for all people. In the same way, when people criticize me for building bridges with Muslims, Hindus, Buddhists, and people of other faiths, I remind them that God's purpose has always been to bless every person on the planet. God told Abraham, "And I will make of you a great nation, and I will bless you and make your name great, so that you will be a blessing. I will bless those who bless you, and him who dishonors you I will curse, and in you all the families of the earth shall be blessed" (Gen. 12:2–3).

The people who will be with us in the new heaven and new earth won't all be white Republicans. They will come from all nations and all cultures. John's record gives us a glimpse: "After this I looked, and behold, a great multitude that no one could number, from every nation, from all tribes and peoples and languages, standing before the throne and before the Lamb, clothed in white robes, with palm branches in their hands, and crying out with a loud voice, 'Salvation belongs to our God who sits on the throne, and to the Lamb!'" (Rev. 7:9–10).

Is there room in your gospel for people of other cultures to come to Christ and experience salvation? Is there room in your heart for their leaders?

FAR AND NEAR

If we engage religious leaders with respect, amazing things can happen. A few years ago, I was in Nepal at a conference of Muslim leaders from Pakistan. We met in Kathmandu in one of the oldest churches in the country. On Saturday, I called a Nepalese friend who years before had taken me hiking to the base camp at Mount Everest. I asked him to pick me up the next morning to take me to church before my flight out that afternoon. As we talked on the phone, one of the imams overheard me. When I hung up, he asked, "Bob, would you take me to the church with you tomorrow? I have never been to a church."

I was very hesitant. I explained, "Yes, you could go, but you need to understand that it won't be like a mosque. It's not as formal. In fact, this church is what we call Pentecostal—it's full of very happy Christians who shout and dance. There will be thousands of them. You can go, but …"

He smiled. "Bob, I want to go!"

I called the pastor to ask if it was okay to bring an imam to church with me the next day. He was glad to have him. But the imam told two other imams, and they asked if they could go too. I had thought two of us could sneak in and sit in the back, but four of us would be much more conspicuous, especially with three of us wearing robes. Before we left the next morning, these three invited more. I left the hotel the next morning with fifteen imams!

I had to hurry to rent a small bus for the drive to the church. On the way, I explained what they would experience in the worship service. I had called the pastor to give him a heads-up, and he provided headsets for each of us with translators for English for me and Urdu for them. Everyone in the church sat on rugs, so at least that part probably felt familiar to the imams. As people in the church clapped to the music, the imams began clapping with them. When people raised their hands in praise and prayer, the imams raised theirs too. I wasn't sure if the scene was a comedy or a drama, but I loved every minute of it.

As the pastor preached, the imams were riveted by every word. I looked to my right at one of the leading Islamic scholars in his country. He was weeping. I leaned over and whispered, "Is something wrong?"

He smiled through his tears and said, "Bob, I sense God in this place!"

I said, "I do too."

I looked to my left and saw another imam with tears running down his cheeks into his beard. I didn't have to ask. I knew he felt the presence of God.

When the service was over and people left the building, the sixteen of us stayed to talk for a while. When no one was around, I asked them, "Has anyone ever explained how you can follow Jesus?"

They all shook their heads, so I asked, "Why do you think they haven't?"

One of them kind of smiled as he said, "They're afraid we'll kill them."

Another one laughed. "And they should be!"

I told them, "Well, I'm not afraid of you killing me, so would you mind if I tell you what we believe about Jesus?"

They all nodded. I continued, "You don't have to agree with me, but here's what we believe." I explained the nature of Christ and the message of the gospel of grace. It was a beautiful moment. When I finished, they put the gospel in the context of the worship they'd just experienced. The message was validated by the love, joy, and hope they'd felt just moments before in the roomful of believers.

Before we walked out, one of them asked, "Bob, would you be willing to spend a week with me at my mosque in Pakistan?"

"Certainly," I answered. "I'm honored."

As I write this, I have just returned from Doha where we had a gathering of top Muslim and Christian leaders from that area. Soon, I'll be going to spend time in Pakistan with the group that invited me. They are introducing me to a wider contingent of leaders in that troubled land. Whoever thought I'd be going to Pakistan to meet with the top Islamic leaders and speaking in their mosque instead of doing traditional mission work? These Islamic imams, the most revered men in their country, have become my friends, and a world of possibilities opened in front of me. I could never have engineered all this. In fact, I couldn't have imagined it. I became friends with these leaders simply by treating them with love and respect.

When I met with these men in Nepal, we talked about the problems of Christians in Muslim countries and Muslims in the United States—and we came up with a plan to address both sides of the cultural divide: I talked to the leaders in Pakistan about the persecution of believers in their country. And later, we brought together twelve leading imams in America with twelve top pastors from the United States to talk about Islamophobia in our country. We went to a dude ranch near Dallas to ride, hunt, and fish for three days. We enjoyed sports, ate well, and talked honestly about the struggles of Muslims in America.

At the conclusion of our three days together, we decided to take small steps to build relationships instead of issuing some kind of white-paper policy statement some might read but few would apply. To pastors and imams across our nation, we made three recommendations:

- Pastors, invite the local imam to your home for dinner, and imams, invite pastors to come for dinner.
- Planned and supported by the church and the mosque, conduct a significant community service project.
- Pastors in America will speak for understanding and against Islamophobia, and imams will take a

stand against religious persecution of Christians
and other religious minorities in countries around
the world.

These are small steps, but they can be the beginning of something
great.

CONSIDER THIS

Who are the leaders of other religions in your community? If you
don't know any of them, who are Jews, Muslims, Hindus, Buddhists,
and people of other religions who work in businesses and restaurants
who can introduce you to the leaders of their religious communities?

In each case, ask for a meeting, introduce yourself, and get to
know the leader. Say something like, "I want you to feel welcome in
our city. Sometimes being in the minority makes people feel lonely
and misunderstood, but I want you to know that I've got your back.
I'm happy to help in any way I can."

We need to be big enough to love people who are different from
us—to respect the differences without painting people as evil. Some
of us can't even respect people who cheer for a different sports team.
Can't we do better than that with the love of Christ and the power
of the Spirit?

Are we more like Jesus, who initiated with every kind of outcast, or
are we more like the Pharisees, who hid behind a facade of superiority toward outsiders?

Is there room in your heart for people of other faiths? If the first Christians had seen Gentiles as inferior and outside the gospel, very few of us would be in the family of God today. They too had their debates about whether to reach out. Thank God they overcame their discrimination and loved people like us.

It's not enough to merely stop condemning "those people" from the pulpit or in private. It's not enough to hold them at arm's length, to shop at their stores but not have any kind of relationship with them. It's not enough to send money for missionaries to reach their families in their countries. Jesus stepped over and around every barrier to connect with outsiders. He became their friend. The leaders of other religions in your community probably haven't had many Christians offer to be their friends. Will you be one of them?

Chapter 8

NO LIMITS

From Exclusive to Inclusive Leadership

From my earliest years, I was taught that the Bible had erected walls to prevent certain people from being in leadership roles. Women, I was sure, had no place at the table. My position has been changing, but I've come to a more open perspective the hard way. When I was sixteen years old, I participated in some speech competitions in high school. During one of the events against another school, I met a girl and led her to the Lord. A few months later, she wrote me a letter and explained, "Bob, God has called me to preach!" She was so excited.

I immediately wrote her and announced, "No, he hasn't!"

She wrote me again and pointed to Deborah, Priscilla, deaconesses, and other women who were leaders and teachers in the Bible. I didn't care what she thought. Though I had never taken a course in New Testament Greek, I was sure the original language didn't mean that! I was sure I was right. Everything in my spiritual culture taught me that God would never allow women to be in leadership positions.

A few years later when I was in seminary, a professor explained in detail why women were denied roles of leadership in the church. A friend leaned over to me and whispered, "I want a lot of women in my church because nobody can clean a commode like a woman!" It was a stage whisper, so everyone could hear. They all laughed ... except for a couple of women in the room.

When my daughter, Jill, was six years old, she came downstairs one day and excitedly told me that she wanted to become a preacher. Instantly, my thoughts flashed back to the scowls of all the pastors and church leaders who would be aghast if they heard my little girl make such a statement.

English evangelist Leonard Ravenhill lived in Lindale, Texas, where my dad pastored First Baptist Church. He came to our church, and I grew up knowing this remarkable man. When I was a college student, I sometimes spent time in his study. He once told me with a wry smile, "You Southern Baptists won't allow women in ministry, so you call them 'missionaries' and send them to die somewhere."

It's not just Southern Baptists. A lot of denominations have put a lid on the role of women. In fact, some pastors in the West get just as worked up about women becoming leaders in their churches as they do about women becoming prostitutes—both career paths are equally appalling! In my tradition a man could have the title of youth pastor, but a woman performing similar duties in the ministry to kids would be called the children's director.

Over the years, my views have been changing. The transition for me began with surprising stories I was hearing about young women in China and other countries who had led house church movements—and many of these women were teenagers. It made me ask myself, *Would I rather they not spread the gospel?* For years, I simply lived with the tension, not knowing how to resolve it.

It became personal for me a few years ago when I was in India with Jossy Chacko. In a remote corner of India, a woman was dying of cancer. Her family and friends exhausted their meager medical resources, so they carried her many miles to a village that had a little hospital. After she was admitted, one of her nurses realized the woman was near death. The nurse was a Christian, so she went to her pastor and asked him to come to the hospital to pray for the sick woman's healing.

The pastor didn't believe in divine healing, so he found excuses to avoid going to the hospital. The nurse, however, refused to let him off the hook. Her persistence forced him to go to the bedside and ask God to do the miraculous in the sick woman's body.

The next day, the doctors found no trace of cancer. The pastor was stunned and confused. He wondered, *How can this happen? I don't even believe God can do something like this!* But God did.

The pastor went to the hospital to meet with the woman. She asked, "What do I do now?"

He explained the gospel to her, and she trusted in Christ. Then she asked the same question again, "What do I do now?"

He told her, "Go home and tell everyone what God has done for you." Before she left the hospital, he gave her a copy of the New Testament in her language and a page of questions. He explained, "If anyone else trusts in Christ, you can use these questions to help you study the Bible together."

About six months later, he received a letter from her. It read, "Some people in our village have believed in Christ. Would you come help us?"

He found reasons why it was impossible to travel to the remote village. Then a few months later, he received another letter. She wrote, "More people have come to Christ. Would you please come to our village to help us?"

This time, he at least responded to her request by sending a note back to her. It said, "I'm sure you're doing fine as you help the people yourself."

After a few more months, she sent him yet another letter requesting his help. She wrote, "We have thirty people who now believe in Jesus, and they need your assistance. Will you please come?"

He told his little church about the request, and the people gave enough money to pay for the pastor's bus ticket to the woman's village. When the bus arrived, he followed the directions to a big open field, where he saw a large crowd of people. They had been waiting for the pastor to come. It turned out that her writing hadn't been very clear. She had written "thirty people," but she had led thirty thousand people to Christ!

Today, this obscure, uneducated woman has one of the most powerful, extensive church-planting movements in India. I've met her. She introduced me to a man she asked to be the executive leader of the movement. He had been a successful scientist for India's nuclear program, but he had found working with her for the cause of Christ to be more thrilling and rewarding than his work as one of his nation's leading scientists.

What would my seminary professor say about this woman's role? What would my friend who whispered that a woman's role is cleaning toilets say about her impact? Did God call her to lead a remarkable movement of the Spirit, or was all of this an illusion or a power trip? Would anyone say she isn't a leader? Would anyone claim she hasn't heard the voice of God? Was she God's plan B because there wasn't a man who responded to his call, or was she his plan A all along?

Her story isn't an isolated one in countries outside the West. I could tell many others of women who have led dynamic churches and powerful movements in China, Indonesia, India, Brazil, and many parts of sub-Saharan Africa.

God's idea of inclusion, though, is much broader than the role of women.

BREAKING DOWN WALLS

One of the most remarkable things about the life of Jesus is that he spent time with people others considered unclean, despised, and inferior. He reached out to care for Samaritans and healed a Roman soldier's slave, he demonstrated God's preferential treatment of the poor, and he elevated the status of women. He broke down the walls of race, class, and gender. Paul reiterated this remarkable change in his letter to the Galatians (who had tried to reinstitute race and class distinctions). He wrote:

> For as many of you as were baptized into Christ have put on Christ. There is neither Jew nor Greek, there is neither slave nor free, there is no male and female, for you are all one in Christ Jesus. And if you are Christ's, then you are Abraham's offspring, heirs according to promise. (Gal. 3:27–29)

I can imagine the people at the church in Galatia falling off their seats as they heard Paul's letter read to them. And I can see them nudge each other and cast eyes at those who had presented themselves as superior because they were Jews, they were rich, and they were men. All believers, Paul was saying, are equal in the eyes of God—no distinctions, no superiority or inferiority, and no limitations.

At Pentecost, 120 people, men and women, waited in the Upper Room for the promise of the Spirit. When the Holy Spirit came, it wasn't only the men who were filled and testified to the greatness of God. Everyone in the room was filled. When we look at the lists of spiritual gifts in Romans, Ephesians, 1 Corinthians, and 1 Peter, we don't see separate lists for men and women, rich and poor, Jews and Gentiles.

The role of women is one of the most contentious in the Western church. There are, of course, specific instructions about limiting the roles of women in particular churches to address specific problems, but the larger, sweeping teaching of the New Testament is the equality of all believers under the headship of Jesus Christ. Let me apply a principle from another field of theology. Pastors, seminary professors, and church leaders disagree about the Bible's teaching of eschatology. Some are premillennial, some are postmillennial, and some are amillennial. The vast majority of us have agreed that our particular position isn't as important as unity in the body of Christ (Phil. 2:1–2; Eph. 4:1–6). In the same way, we need to stop getting so worked up over the role of women in church leadership.

In the West we often categorize theological positions as "either/or," whether we're describing the second coming of Christ, the role of the Holy Spirit, or any of hundreds of other topics. However, I believe we can find a new way of crafting the conversation about women in ministry. Theologically conservative pastors and seminary professors are found on both sides of the issue, with a strong biblical basis for each position. Instead of separating into complementarian and egalitarian camps, we should ask the Holy Spirit to guide people in ministry, including women who want to serve in leadership roles.

Should we have qualifications? Of course. If women feel called, if they aren't in rebellion and don't have any disqualifying character problems, if they want to glorify God, if they want to use their God-given gifts to serve others, and if they have a track record of hearing and obeying the voice of God, why don't we trust the Spirit to guide them into a role in ministry? If there is neither Jew nor Greek, bond nor free, we might also conclude there is neither male nor female.

If you disagree with the egalitarian view or the complementarian, be gracious; don't attack, accuse, and belittle. We need to acknowledge we're all in process. Last year a major group of conservative young pastors in the United States told their constituency they were rethinking their views of women in ministry. They described the value they and their churches gained from women in leadership roles. They weren't ready to have women as pastors, but they realized a predominately masculine view of roles in church isn't relationally healthy or theologically accurate.

As we look at the church around the world, we can celebrate the fact that God is using women to accomplish amazing things for his glory. I want to lean toward freedom instead of restriction. If I err, I want to err on the side of letting more people love and serve God rather than being narrow and limiting what God might do.

At a major conference for church planters, the leaders of the event asked several of us to stay after our last session to pray with people and anoint them with oil. A young woman and her husband came up to me. She was weeping with excitement. She told me, "I'm so ready to start this church. Would you ask God to use me?" It was such a joy to anoint her and pray for her and her husband as she launched a new church with his support. I asked God to bless their socks off!

THE BEGINNING OF CHANGE

The divisions, the walls, the boxes, and the superiority and inferiority are as old as human nature, but Jesus and the early church powerfully addressed the problem. The key to the launch and expansion of the church was the breaking down of barriers so that both Jews and Gentiles became equal partners in God's kingdom; slaves and free people were considered equally valuable, equally gifted, and equally qualified for leadership; and women were elevated to an equal status with men instead of considered property. Read Acts and the letters through this lens, and you might be amazed at what you find.

After Pentecost, the number of believers began to explode. Thousands came to Christ, including some of the priests. (I've always wondered if some were those who had been in the temple when the veil was torn as Jesus died.) Of course, believers are still very human, and resentment surfaced because the Greek widows felt overlooked when resources were distributed. The problem must have been significant, because it got the attention of the twelve apostles. To solve the dilemma, the apostles asked all the believers to come up with a solution. The gathering of disciples appointed seven servants, dea-cons, to handle food distribution. The seven men, however, were all Greek. To make sure the problem was solved with the utmost honor and authenticity, they appointed Greeks to distribute food to both Greek widows and Hebrew widows. The racial and ethnic divide had been bridged.

We often read Acts 6 as the story of the inception of the role of deacons or the establishment of church polity, but it's more than that. It's a statement of who matters in the church—it's a statement of racial equality. The Hebrew majority treated the Greek minority with grace, love, and honor. They could have selected a proportion-ate number of deacons to represent each ethnic group, maybe five to two or six to one, but instead, they went to the greatest lengths to promote ethnic and racial unity—all seven were Greek (Acts 6:1–7).

One of the biggest questions in the early church was whether Gentiles would have to become Jewish in order to be Christians. Would they have to be circumcised and obey the law to be in the family of God? The Jerusalem council in Acts 15 wrestled with this problem. After listening to the debate, the leaders decided it was God's will to accept Gentiles as equals in God's family. To be sure there was no misunderstanding, they sent letters to all the churches with mixed races. When the church in Antioch, the first stop for Paul and Barnabas, read the letter, "they rejoiced because of its encourage-ment" (Acts 15:31). We can almost hear a sigh of relief.

In the West, we've built our churches around target groups and our congregations have become largely homogeneous instead of diverse. In the 1950s, church-growth expert Dr. Donald McGavran suggested this strategy for reaching segments of communities with the gospel. In God's kingdom, however, the target group is *all people* in the community. To accomplish this feat, we may have to be as bold as the early church and make dramatic decisions to show we value those who feel second class or are easily ignored. Actually, McGavran warned that targeting homogeneous groups could lead to a lack of diversity. He was right; it has. Leading pastors in the United States, including Mark DeYmaz, Efrem Smith, Bryan Loritts, and Derwin Gray, have planted multiethnic *churches* that have grown. These leaders are now starting *movements* of multiethnic churches.

NOT A DEBATE IN THE EAST

In many parts of the world, Western colonialization has created a dichotomy between the indigenous people and the new ruling powers, the haves and the have-nots, the whites and the people of any other ethnic background. Quite often, these walls were added to the existing divisions between tribes (in many cases, literal tribes) that had, for generations, been suspicious of each other and hated each other. In this atmosphere of fierce segmentation and power grabs, the gospel of inclusion has shown a very different way to relate.

Today, migration is changing the face of the globe. In fact, in some countries such as the United Arab Emirates, the native population of Arab Muslims is far outnumbered by those who have come from Africa, the Philippines, and India seeking good-paying jobs. In other parts of the world, walls have come down for very different reasons. Tens of thousands of Libyans and Syrians are risking their lives in leaky boats in their attempt to flee the violence in their home countries for the safety of European shores. And millions of people in the war-ravaged Middle East have been displaced as they look for protection. In a *Washington Post* article, Wes Granberg-Michaelson examined the impact of immigration and reported:

> The striking religious factor is that overall, about 105 million who have migrated are Christians—a significantly higher percentage than their 33 percent of the world's population. Sociologists report that the process of immigration typically increases the intensity of religious faith—whatever its form—of those persons crossing borders of nations and cultures. Fresh spiritual vitality in both North America and Europe is being fueled by the process of global migration.[1]

When different races, ethnic groups, and cultures are thrown together, they are suspicious and competitive. It's human nature. But when the gospel breaks down the walls that divide people, they find ways to accept and even celebrate differences instead of despising one another.

When civil war came to Nicaragua, Mario Vega's cell church was dispersed in the chaos of destruction. Like the early church that was scattered by persecution and grew wider and deeper, Mario's people have been beacons of love and hope where they've taken new roots, and the number of believers has grown.

Throughout the world, all three barriers are being torn down by the grace of God. Races are learning to love one another, the poor are valued, and women are elevated as equals.

CHANGES IN OUR CHURCH

We have a lot to learn from our brothers and sisters overseas. Since I've gotten to know these pastors in the Global Collaborative Community, I see racism, class distinctions, and gender inequality more clearly in the American church … and in *my* church. I realized that many traditionally white churches in America are more than willing to send money to a struggling African American or Hispanic church in another part of the city, and they tolerate those people coming to their services, but they are horrified that "one of them" would be put in leadership over them. In other words, paternalism is acceptable but equality isn't.

When people from other cultures are fully integrated into the body and the leadership of a church, radical change occurs. Are we willing to let that happen? Do we *want* it to happen? Too often, we want our comfortable worship style more than we want our church to represent the wide, messy, and beautiful kingdom of God. We want leaders we know and who share our history instead of having to trust people whose traditions are very different. We want to look down the pew and see people who are just like us so we can relax and feel at home; but we don't realize our true home in the new heaven and new earth will look like the color wheel at Sherwin-Williams— and white won't be the dominant color!

As I've wrestled with the traditional limits on race, class, and gender at our church, I've taken our people in a new direction. I've become "that guy" my seminary professor warned our class against. We now have women in pastoral roles—with pastoral titles—and they teach and preach as well as lead. On our small elder board, we have a man who is Hispanic-Palestinian. Our church staff is a broad mix of ethnicities. We want it to reflect our community, not the ratio of our current attenders. One of our staff members is African American, Japanese, and German. (I hoped we could also find some South American heritage in her, but no luck.)

In past years, we had ministries for the poor in our metropolitan area and we felt good about our outreach programs. But recently, I've realized that's paternalism, not kingdom unity in the body of Christ. It's not enough to send resources and help believers start churches. Jesus sat with the poor, ate with them, and touched them to heal them. He delighted in them, and they knew it. Can I say that poor people and those of other races and cultures know I delight in them? Do they feel treasured and honored when they walk through the doors of my office, my home, or my church? At NorthWood, do we take special pains to be sure they feel comfortable, not in a power play to show we're better, but out of genuine love and respect?

When I started traveling around the world to meet with the global pastors and speak in domains in different countries, it dawned on me that I was reaching out more to people on the other side of the globe than those on the other side of my own city. I had neglected African Americans, Hispanics, Indians, Vietnamese, Muslims, and many other ethnic groups in this area. But I didn't want to come across as "big brother is here to pat you on the head and fix your problems." I wanted to engage them, listen to their hearts, respect them, honor them, involve them, and have the same qualifications of leadership for them as I had for the white people in our congregation. No exclusions. No limits.

As I've gotten to know more African Americans, I've realized why the church has virtually no credibility in the racial struggles in our country. We've marginalized ourselves by our smug attitudes and self-righteous blaming—not all of us, of course, but enough of us that we've lost our collective voice of love, hope, and reconciliation. When I realized the depth of the racial divide in our culture, I began to speak about the power of the gospel to build bridges. Many of the Anglos in our church took me aside, in person or by email, and warned me I shouldn't draw attention to or talk about it. The African Americans and Hispanics also took me aside, but they thanked me for talking about the truth. I realized the kingdom of God is far bigger, far more colorful, and far more diverse than the narrow version I'd lived in all my life. And I loved it!

You always pay a price for change, and we've paid one for our commitment to inclusion. Not many left our church when we put women in leadership. There were a few ripples, but most people felt comfortable with the new direction. But being inclusive about race and class caused far more disputes. We've had a number of people leave our church, including some of our big donors. On the other side, many more ethnic minorities have found a home with us. They don't always have as much money to contribute, but they have a ton of heart. I'll be honest with you: the loss of people and contributions has caused some headaches, but the benefits of having a kingdom-minded church outweigh the deficits any day.

BOLD STEPS

Even if you hold a theologically complementarian view of the role of women, I want to still push you to consider how to let women play a more significant role in shaping the culture and the message of your church. Move toward inclusion. And be honest with yourself. Don't be afraid of losing control to women. Be man enough to let them have a voice. Don't worry about women's lib. Sure, a few women want power instead of wanting to serve, but I know plenty of men who also fit that description. God is calling people, both men and women, not because they have something to prove, but because they have a lot to give to him, to their community, and to God's people. Even if you don't give them titles or a seat at the leadership table, find ways to listen to them and honor them.

In our efforts to address racial inequality, we've had more than our share of conferences in which we've heard blacks, Hispanics, and whites talk about the issue for hours. Typically, all the speakers are from fairly homogeneous churches, and they talk about the problem without offering kingdom solutions. It's time to be more intentional and to push the commitment for change down to the churches, churches like yours and mine. We need to hire staff and select key volunteer leaders based on the ethnic diversity of our communities, not our current population on Sunday morning. We need to change our worship style to reflect the community instead of our traditions. McGavran's principle of the "homogeneous unit" is designed to shape our evangelistic efforts, not how to grow a church that reflects the diversity of the community. He never intended it to exclude anyone.

We need to avoid being paternalistic in our relationship with poor people. Our church started churches in the inner city for African Americans and Hispanics. There's nothing wrong with that, but many of them wanted to come to NorthWood because they wanted to hear more about the kingdom. They bring incredible value to our church.

When I preached a series on racial diversity and inclusion, I asked one of our members, Jose, to share his story. He talked about hearing the gospel at NorthWood and the joy he'd found in knowing the Lord. He was honest that he was initially hesitant to come to our church when a friend first invited him. He didn't want to go to a church "with a lot of gringos." He explained that he came from a rough background and he was sure he wouldn't fit in with rich white people from the suburbs. But, he told us, when he walked in, he felt welcomed and loved. He opened his heart to the gospel, and his life was radically changed.

Jose's three sons were born in the United States, but he wasn't. Some of our members got involved to help him become a citizen. The immigration debate has many sides, but the people of NorthWood had seen Jose come to faith in Christ, and they have loved him, his wife, and his kids for the past three years. They wanted to help him become a legal citizen. Jose and his wife have brought many of their friends to NorthWood. I can't tell you what it does to a pastor when you're worshipping and you look up and you see all the races, men and women, worshipping at the top of their lungs with one voice. An ardent Anglo Texan told me, "I've always had a stereotype of illegals, but Jose has broken the mold. He's my friend. I trust him. Maybe I need to rethink my perspective on immigration."

Jose's testimony was a turning point in the lives of many in our church. They had built a relationship with Jose without knowing his whole story. They liked him when they assumed he was a "law-abiding citizen," but now, they had to process new facts about him. They suddenly had to decide: Do I see Jose as a political problem, or do I see him as a brother in Christ? Their answer said everything about their view of the kingdom.

Jesus breaks down the walls separating people according to gender, race, and class. The kingdom shatters presumptions and prejudices, and it builds community, purpose, and love. The church on the other side of the world is leading the way to tear down those walls, and we'd be wise to follow suit. Our schools, sports, the arts, and government have all desegregated, but the faces in most of our churches—white, black, and Hispanic—are usually a single color. In most communities, our churches are more segregated than the neighborhoods around them. If the cross was the great leveler and caused Paul to recognize that it was for both Jew and Greek (race), male and female (gender), slave and free (class), what right do I have to erect walls that Jesus died to destroy?

My friend, our penchant for preference needs to change.

CONSIDER THIS

As you read this chapter, was your heart thrilled with the idea of tearing down walls, or were you thinking of excuses to stay with the status quo?

Stop limiting the gospel in relation to women, the different races in your community, and the poor. Lean into inclusion. Don't be paternalistic. Push beyond it, and welcome people as brothers and sisters in the kingdom. You'll be getting in good practice for the new heaven and new earth.

Part II

KINGDOM HEARTS

Chapter 9

ABANDONED

From Safety to Radical Obedience

Self-abandonment and humility aren't cause and effect; they're mutually stimulating and progressive. They both begin with a growing awareness of God's greatness and our smallness, the wonder of God's grace and the darkness of our hearts, being amazed that the God of glory would go to great lengths to forgive us, adopt us, and make us his partners in the greatest work mankind has ever known: restoring a lost and broken world. In the next two chapters, we'll look at both of these traits of a person who has a heart for God and his kingdom. First, we'll examine the choice of radical obedience over playing it safe.

How seriously do we take Jesus and his calling to be fully his? How much do we value comfort, prestige, approval, and having nice things more than we value Christ and his kingdom? In the West, most Christians believe God's job is to give them a happy, prosperous life.[1] In a piercing and poignant observation, psychologist Larry Crabb observed that most American Christians see God as a "specially attentive waiter." When he gives us good service, we may give him a tip of thanks. But if his service disappoints us, we complain.[2] God exists, we're convinced, to make our lives comfortable and affluent.

Christian leaders from other parts of the world, at least the ones I have the privilege of knowing, have a very different view of God, the purpose of the kingdom, and the sacrifice Christians must make to advance the kingdom. In the West, our goal is a "balanced Christian life"; in the East, the goal is to be fully abandoned to Jesus Christ and his cause because he is worthy of our complete love and loyalty. In his letter to the Philippians, Paul mirrored the attitude and actions of my friends in the Global Collaborative Community:

> But whatever gain I had, I counted as loss for the sake of Christ. Indeed, I count everything as loss because of the surpassing worth of knowing Christ Jesus my Lord. For his sake I have suffered the loss of all things and count them as rubbish, in order that I may gain Christ and be found in him, not having a righteousness of my own that comes from the law, but that which comes through faith in Christ, the righteousness from God that depends on faith—that I may know him and the power of his resurrection, and may share his sufferings, becoming like him in his death, that by any means possible I may attain the resurrection from the dead. (Phil. 3:7–11)

For Americans to be willing to suffer for Christ, we need a very different view of him, of ourselves, and of his purpose for our lives.

To these global leaders, sharing in the sufferings of Christ isn't an anomaly; it's normal. In many of these countries, the choice to become a Christian comes with the threat of losing your job, being shunned by your family, being thrown in jail, being tortured, or losing your life. Christian leaders often live with death threats. I've seen, though, that when people are faced with the actual prospect of dying for their faith, they become disciples who are radically different from those in the West who only follow God if he makes their lives comfortable, prosperous, and fun.

If believers have to trust God for survival, they're much more willing to trust him to speak to them from his Word, much more willing to trust God for supernatural healing and power, and much more willing to demonstrate a deeper, stronger, sacrificial love for others, including enemies. And people whose lives are threatened don't quibble as much about fine points of theology. They're glad to have any allies they can find!

We have a lot to learn from our friends in the East. Since 9/11, the nightly news has carried a steady stream of horrifying videos and reports about Islamic extremists. They have bombed, shot, beheaded, and terrified people on virtually every continent. My global friends who serve in countries with at least a large minority of Muslims are often targets because they've led so many people to Christ. I asked one pastor how he handles death threats. He answered, "Bob, when you accept Jesus, you accept all of him. Every day, I know that my response to opposition will encourage or discourage the people I lead."

At a large conference for pastors, a woman had a prophetic word. She stood up and said only, "Danger! Danger!" I was sitting with Sam Sung Kim, who plants churches in Central Asia. He looked at me and smiled. I gave him a look that asked, *What are you saying?* He whispered, "Bob, when has there *not* been danger? This is nothing new."

Jossy Chacko has been very successful as an entrepreneur and church planter, but he hasn't forgotten the cost of following Christ. He carries a Bible that had been owned by a young pastor whose church in India grew and became a threat to militant Hindus. The militants murdered him, and the pastor's wife gave Jossy the blood-stained Bible. Jossy treasures it because it reminds him of the price this young pastor and his family paid to serve Christ.

As I write these words, I just received a list of the countries where men and women are imprisoned because they claim the name of Jesus Christ. This cost and this sacrifice are incomprehensible in America, but not in other parts of the world.

Africa has seen more than its share of violence, including Al-Shabaab's 2013 attack on a mall in Nairobi that killed thirty-nine and wounded more than 150. Throughout Kenya, people live on edge. Christians wonder if they'll be the next targets of the extremists, and peaceful Muslims wonder if they'll be marginalized because of their violent brothers' actions.

Joseph Maisha has stepped into this quagmire of hatred and despair to offer a kingdom perspective full of love, hope, and wisdom. When he became a Christian, he immediately began telling others about the love and forgiveness he found in Christ. The response was decidedly mixed: some trusted in Jesus, while others chased Joseph and beat him with sticks. Today, as a pastor in Mombasa, he knows that his leadership in the Christian faith makes him a big target for the extremists. He and his family have been threatened. His courage to love and lead, however, doesn't come from his personality or political convictions. His abandonment to God stems from a deep, abiding sense of God's calling. He explained:

> It's easy to be afraid. I look at God's words to Jeremiah. God called him as a prophet: "Before I formed you in the womb I knew you, and before you were born I consecrated you; I appointed you a prophet to the nations." But Jeremiah was a young man who was very afraid. He found excuses to stay safe instead of following God's calling. He told God, "I do not know how to speak, for I am only a youth." But God responded, "Do not say, 'I am only a youth'; for to all to whom I send you, you shall go, and whatever I command you, you shall speak. Do not be afraid of them, for I am with you to deliver you, declares the LORD." Jeremiah wasn't going on his own authority, for his own glory, or in his own power. The Lord touched Jeremiah's mouth and told him, "Behold, I have put my words in your mouth. See, I have set you this day over nations and over kingdoms, to pluck up and to break down, to destroy and to overthrow, to build and to plant" (Jer. 1:5–10).
>
> In the same way, I know that God has called me to serve him and obey him. Because he has called me, I don't doubt him when I face adversity. It's part of his calling. Many pastors are afraid of

what will happen to them if they face opposition. They need to understand that this work isn't about them; it's about God. Who am I? I'm only a servant, but he has put his words in my mouth. When I speak, I say what the Holy Spirit has given me to tell them. I don't go to them with my agenda. When people think we have our own agenda, they think we're trying to control them. God has called me to Mombasa, to a difficult place. That's his choice, and I simply respond in obedience. I don't worry about my safety, and I don't worry about the results. Jesus must produce the results, and nothing is impossible for him. God is watching to see what we really want. Are we establishing his kingdom or our kingdoms? We must be humble and patient, and then God will work. I tell pastors, "Don't be impatient, and don't give up. Don't blame yourself when people don't respond. Your ministry is not about you; it's about Jesus Christ."

I'm amazed, inspired, and humbled by the faith of Christians in countries where believers pay a steep price for following Jesus. A friend of mine, Chris Seiple, leads an organization called the Institute for Global Engagement.[3] Chris asked me to be part of a delegation working with the state departments of Vietnam and the United States on the issue of religious freedom. Vietnam's leaders wanted to join the World Trade Organization, and one of the requirements was addressing human rights. We attended the official meetings, and we then traveled to another part of the country to meet with a group of local pastors.

Several of the pastors we met previously had been arrested and put in prison for years. They had suffered, and their families had suffered. When they were released, however, they didn't hide from danger. They took up where they had left off, leading their churches under the constant threat of being arrested again. In their stories, I didn't detect even a hint of self-pity or complaint. They considered it a privilege to suffer for Jesus. As the pastors described the suffering, constant threats, and imprisonment they had endured, my heart broke. I had to leave the room. I went into a bathroom and sobbed.

God is using these incredible leaders to bring thousands, actually tens of thousands, to Christ. Their networks of cell churches are enormous, but their success is built on the back of suffering, not plenty. People in America have never heard of these leaders, but I have heard their stories, and I have realized the yawning gap between their commitment to Christ and my own. Meeting them inspires me and humbles me.

CLEARER LENSES

The pastors in Vietnam and my global friends have shown me what it means to truly live with self-abandoned trust in God. From them, I've learned to see two familiar passages through clearer lenses. Jesus drew a stark contrast between loyalty to him and caring more about popularity, wealth, and comfort: "If anyone would come after me, let him deny himself and take up his cross and follow me. For whoever would save his life will lose it, but whoever loses his life for my sake will find it. For what will it profit a man if he gains the whole world and forfeits his soul? Or what shall a man give in return for his soul?" (Matt. 16:24–26). Similarly, in his letter to the Galatians, Paul said the only life worth living is the one that is fully Christ's. He wrote, "I have been crucified with Christ. It is no longer I who live, but Christ who lives in me. And the life I now live in the flesh I live by faith in the Son of God, who loved me and gave himself for me" (Gal. 2:20).

Years ago I heard someone say that we're not ready to live for a cause if we're not ready to die for it. The statement may seem trite, but it's true. As I've gotten to know my friends from the most difficult parts of the world, I've seen this principle lived out. These amazing people echo Paul's heart when he said farewell to the Ephesian elders, men he had loved and led for almost three years. He told them, "And now, behold, I am going to Jerusalem, constrained by the Spirit, not knowing what will happen to me there, except that the Holy Spirit testifies to me in every city that imprisonment and afflictions await me. But I do not account my life of any value nor as precious to myself, if only I may finish my course and the ministry that I received from the Lord Jesus, to testify to the gospel of the grace of God" (Acts 20:22–24).

God used this passage in my life to radically reorient my purpose and direction. Our church had moved to a new location, and I was sure we'd grow a lot. We didn't. This was the point when the Spirit of God asked me, "Bob, when will Jesus be enough for you?" At that moment, I began to understand the greatness of the kingdom, as well as the cost of the kingdom. I asked God for a bigger vision, one that was far beyond the walls of our church. In that season, our church began connecting with churches in Vietnam, but because we went through the front door, the government connected us with them—we weren't manipulating the system or doing anything illegal. This passage reminded me that sacrifice is essential if we pursue the kingdom. This passage gave me courage when I began traveling to Afghanistan. And God used this passage in a conversation with my daughter, Jill, when she was in the eighth grade and wondered why her father was going to the most dangerous places on earth to build God's kingdom.

When building my church and advancing my reputation were the focus of my life, all of my "good" activities as a pastor were actually self-serving. God had to shake up my world with failure, and then he had to expose me to the most courageous men and women on earth as they serve him in Syria, Iraq, Iran, Egypt, Indonesia, Central Asia, India, and other difficult parts of the world. People there need Jesus, and God's people are paying a high price to tell them about him.

THE EYES OF JESUS

The pastors in these countries don't hate their persecutors. They see them through the eyes of Jesus, and they love them. These brave pastors look for God to work even in the darkest hours. When the twenty-one Coptic Christians were paraded to the shore of the Mediterranean and beheaded, a godly man tweeted, "May one of these men of ISIS become a Paul for the church today." That's the ability to see enemies through the loving, hopeful eyes of our Savior, who died for the ungrateful, the ungodly, the vicious, and the hopeless. By the way, I've met people in different parts of the world who decided to follow Jesus because of the courage of those twenty-one martyrs from Egypt. One man told me, "Why did they die? It made me wonder what was it about their faith." The nobility and faith of the martyrs inspired faith in this man and others like him.

In my conversation with Jill about suffering and sacrifice, I wanted her to know that if something happens to me, I want her to keep loving Muslims. I want them to matter to her because she's convinced they matter to God.

To truly love people from different cultures, we have to be with them, to get to know them, to see their hearts. The people in our church didn't really love the people of Vietnam until we went there and spent time with them. It's the same with our love for Muslims, for Hindus, and for people of different ethnicities in our own community. As long as we remain at arm's length (or ocean's length), our hearts can remain cool and we can objectify people as "them." But when we get to know these people, we begin to see them through the eternally loving, optimistic, courageous eyes of Jesus.

Too often, Western church leaders have the wrong metric. We're possessive of the people who come to our services, and we do what we can to keep them coming back week after week. One American pastor commented, "I'm always only two bad sermons away from a mass exodus." We view any activities that might detract from our attendance and finances as threats. Any distraction—such as a radical commitment to the kingdom and global missions—is a serious threat to our popularity and our numbers. That's a very different threat than the ones my global friends face every day!

Suffering, and the risk of suffering, reveals the true nature of our commitment to Christ. After Job had suffered the loss of everything he held dear, he asked God, "Why?" Instead of answering his question, God revealed his greatness and sovereignty. Job was blown away. In response, he replied, "I know that you can do all things, and that no purpose of yours can be thwarted" (Job 42:2). Loss, heartache, and false accusations from his "friends" had driven Job to the throne of grace. There, he found a great and wise God—not answers to his specific questions, but the ultimate answer. He became convinced that God was supremely trustworthy, even if he didn't understand what God was doing in his life. When he was amazed at the greatness of God, he could rest.

Every great leader in the Bible came to a point of reckoning. God brought Abraham, Moses, the prophets, Peter, Paul, and all the rest to a point of self-abandonment so they would turn to him to be filled and overflowing. In America, we hate suffering. We see it as sub-Christian, abnormal, and wrong. But it's God's divine curriculum to refine us and focus our hearts more fully on him so that we love him more than we love his blessings or the comforts of this world.

David was a great warrior and king. As he defended Israel, enemies often attacked him and his people. In a wonderful declaration of his deepest desires, he wrote:

> One thing have I asked of the LORD,
> that will I seek after:
> that I may dwell in the house of the LORD
> all the days of my life,
> to gaze upon the beauty of the LORD
> and to inquire in his temple. (Ps. 27:4)

I have to ask myself, and I'll ask you:

- Is the Lord beautiful to us? Is he more lovely and awe inspiring than anything else in our lives?
- Do we find him to be beautiful in himself so that we marvel at him like we marvel at a gorgeous landscape, a symphony, or a piece of art, or do we more often consider him to be useful in helping us accomplish our goals and fulfill our desires?
- Is he our wonder or our waiter?

Seeking the answers to these questions may take some time to dig beneath superficial responses, excuses, and denial, but it's an important exercise. God will use any means possible to get our attention and wake us up to his greatness and grace. Only then will we be more obsessed with him than with our success and prestige. Only then will our thoughts naturally drift to his beauty instead of our worries or daydreaming about hitting it big. Only then will we say "Wow!" about him instead of "Wow!" about our competition. We have to be more obsessed with Jesus than our safety, our bank account, or our numbers last Sunday.

In a culture of celebrity pastors, we want fans. If that's our goal, our lives are all about image management, not honoring God and expanding his kingdom. In this environment, it's easy for the people in our churches to mistake loyalty to us and our churches with devotion to Jesus. They're not the same, not even close. We don't find two different standards for self-denial, self-sacrifice, and devotion to Christ, one in America and the other throughout the rest of the world. He's the same shepherd, and we're the same kind of sheep. In America, we're more insulated from suffering than in most of the rest of the world, so our devotion is often untested and unproven. We haven't paid a very high price, so we aren't as invested in Christ and his kingdom. Dietrich Bonhoeffer was right: "When Christ calls a man, he bids him come and die. It may be a death like that of the first disciples who had to leave home and work to follow him, or it may be a death like Luther's, who had to leave the monastery and go out into the world. But it is the same death every time—death in Jesus Christ, the death of the old man at his call."[4]

When we experience persecution (or at least opposition), God accomplishes three important goals in our lives:

- The difficulty *clarifies* our beliefs, passions, and loyalties. We can stop and ask ourselves, "What do I really believe about God, about my purpose in life, and about the people who are harassing me? Do I really believe Jesus died on the cross for Muslims, gays, inner-city black men, immigrants, and any others who might be easily written off? Do I believe Jesus loves them as much as he loves me? Do I believe it enough to die for Jesus, to suffer for him, or at least to be inconvenienced for him?"

- Opposition *purifies* our hearts by burning off the impurities of selfishness, pride, and irrational fear. Heartache has a way of cutting through the surface layers of our lives to expose our true desires. Do we really want God and his kingdom more than anything in the world? When we brought John Murray to be the worship pastor of our church, he came from the Potter's House. His music didn't come from a white suburban culture, and consequently, some of our people felt uncomfortable with it. I asked them, "Is the kingdom of God and the ability to reach out to everyone in our community more important than your comfort level with a particular worship style?" To many, that's a very difficult question to answer.

• Struggles can *propel multiplication* in a congregation, as hearts are opened for people who were formerly outside their comfort zones. In our church, our ministry to Hispanics, Muslims, Indians, and many other ethnic groups has exploded, even as we've been viciously attacked by some who see these people as enemies instead of those for whom Christ died.

A couple of years ago when we were making our major shift toward minorities, I went to the local mall to buy a shirt to wear on Easter Sunday. A woman there recognized me. She stopped me and said, "Pastor Bob!"

I replied, "How did you know I'm a pastor?"

She explained, "I came to the event at your church when you invited all the Muslims in town." She smiled, leaned toward me, and almost whispered, "Don't tell my imam, but I come often to your church. I'll see you on Easter!"

When we're thrilled with Jesus, he always leads us to care about people he loves, but we may pay a price for it. When I started building relationships with Muslims, people went on Twitter and Facebook to say the nastiest things about our church and me. I was stunned by the attacks. During the worst of it, my son laughed and told me, "Dad, when I get discouraged, I google your name and read some of the horrible things people have posted about you. They don't have a clue who you are or what you're doing! If you can put up with that, I can put up with the problems in my life."

ABANDONED IN AMERICA

So, what does it look like to be fully abandoned to God in a self-indulgent culture? We aren't threatened with persecution or death, so what does it mean to live courageously in America for the Savior? It means we love to the extreme. It means when we don't get our way, we don't act like victims. We don't complain, we don't blame, and we don't withdraw. Instead, we are grateful for all we have, for the incredible opportunities God has given us, and for the freedom to live without fear. And in our gratitude, we invest our hearts and resources in the people Jesus loves.

If Jesus were living in your community, whom would he love? He'd love the Muslims, the Cambodians, the refugees from Somalia, and the immigrants who crossed the border—whether they have green cards or not. He would love the lost and the least, the homeless and the hungry, the sick and the prisoners—not with a paternalistic passing gesture, but with tender, engaged, warm, tenacious, and wise compassion. God has given me a special love for Muslims. There are almost two billion of them in the world, and some of them live in every community in America. If we reach out and love the Muslim immigrants here, a few of them may go back home and open doors for the gospel.

If you want to love like Jesus loves, reach out to gay people. Again, not to correct them or rebuke them or to offer them a program to change them so you'll feel more comfortable or powerful, but to love them as they are, with no expectations or demands. Have them in your home. Show respect for their hopes and dreams. Engage them in meaningful, not demeaning, conversations. You can tell them you don't agree with them but you want to be their friend.

Put your kids in the public schools. Don't retreat to a cocoon of a safe environment. Equip your kids to think, pray, and act from a kingdom perspective. Don't hide them from a sinful society; help them be radical disciples in the public arena. Teach them to stand up for Jesus in a fallen world. Then, when they graduate and enter the world, they'll be able to relate to people with a wealth of wisdom, maturity, and love.

I was brought up in a very evangelistic denomination; we talked often and always about our love for lost people. In recent years, I'd have to say that this assessment wasn't true ... at least for me and maybe for many more than me. We love the *idea* of evangelism, and we love the *concept* of lost people of other faiths and other lifestyles coming to Christ. We just don't want those people in our churches. It's just too messy. We were glad to send missionaries to the far reaches of the map, but we wanted our churches to be full of people who looked like us, thought like us, talked like us, and voted like us, and by the way, sang like us and cooked like us. We wanted to be known as people who reached the world, but we didn't want the world to show up at our churches. And we couldn't imagine those people actually being our friends.

Jesus was vilified for loving the social and cultural outcasts, the rank sinners, the despised and forsaken, the demon possessed, the sick and blind, and all those who had no standing in their community. Are we being vilified for loving too many too much? If not, are we truly representing Christ and his kingdom? I'm not suggesting that opposition is the measuring stick of our devotion, because the opposition we experience may be the result of us simply being offensive and rude. Christ's kingdom is just the opposite; it's full of kindness—care for the oppressed, compassion for the needy, and love for the outcasts, whether they are rich like Zacchaeus or poor like the lepers.

Are the rigid, religious people attacking you because you love "the wrong people"? What are you giving up in terms of reputation and resources to care for outcasts, misfits, and the forgotten?

One of the most common excuses for maintaining distance is "I can't be everywhere and help everybody." That's so lame. No, you can't be everywhere, but you can show up *somewhere*. And no, you can't help everybody, but you can help *somebody*. And it must be more than a token wave at the crushing needs of people across town and across the globe. Caring for us cost Jesus his life; caring for others will cost us at least something. We are the richest nation and the richest church on earth. God has put a wealth of resources in our hands. We may not face persecution like some believers in the world, but we face accountability: "Everyone to whom much was given, of him much will be required" (Luke 12:48).

One of the marks of a life abandoned to God is the willingness to move beyond the safety of our tribes. Jesus stepped out of the security and glory of heaven to live and die for sinners like you and me. If we know even a little of the depth of his grace, we'll step out and take some risks to love people who are very different from us.

What scares us most when we think about going to the darkest, most violent parts of the world? Losing our lives. What scares us most when we think about breaking the mold and loving people from other cultures on the other side of the city? Losing our reputations, especially among the power brokers in our tribes. Unless we love Jesus more than we love safety and applause, we'll stay stuck in passivity and self-righteousness. We'll analyze, study, and observe people in other cultures, but we won't really love them. Jesus was called "a friend of sinners." Who calls us their friends?

Who are the groups of people who are coming to your church because you've taken such a loving, courageous, bold stand to reach out to them? What price are you paying to love them? It's one thing to market your church to your community and hope "the right people" come. It's a very different thing to represent Jesus to every corner of your community.

BOLD AND HUMBLE

Some people might wonder how a leader can be a radical activist with a bold kingdom vision and still be humble and gracious. Aren't the two mutually exclusive, or at least hard to reconcile? No, not in the least. The global leaders who have become my friends hold both in their hands. They see their calling, their vision, and their resources as gifts from God to be used for his glory. They have the unspeakable privilege of being his beloved children and his honored partners in the greatest endeavor the world has ever known: redeeming and restoring a lost and broken world. In the same breath, they echo Caleb's boldness: "Give me that mountain!" (Josh. 14:12, paraphrase), as well as David's humble sense of wonder as he prayed to God, "What is man that you are mindful of him?" (Ps. 8:4).

Our deepest desires show us where we're alive and where we're dead: delighting in the greatness and grace of God and wanting to honor him above all, or longing for power, prestige, and possessions. Which pursuit revs our engines and makes us feel alive? It's not an easy question to answer.

Jesus invites us to take up our cross of self-denial, but we'll be motivated to take it up only if we realize he has first taken up his cross to pay the ultimate price for us. When we find Jesus to be the most beautiful, valuable wonder of our lives, we'll have the security to let our hidden desires surface. We may find more fear, resentment, and pride than we ever imagined, but now we can't live with it any longer. We want him more than safety, we want him more than popularity, and we want him more than always being right. We want him more than anything, and gradually, the love we experience becomes the love we express. We'll be freed up to be bold, but not for self-promotion. And we'll be freed to love, but not out of a need to manipulate or impress.

Loving Jesus supremely doesn't cause our fears to vanish. Quite often he leads us into places where our fears multiply, but he promises to be with us there. Courage is managed fear, not the absence of fear. Sometimes when my flight takes off from Dallas–Fort Worth Airport, I wonder if I'll be coming home again. I frequently travel to places where Christians are imprisoned, tortured, and killed. I have no assurance of protection, but I have great assurance that the journey is right. My prayer is "God, don't let me die stupidly or meaninglessly. Don't let me do something really dumb that gets me killed, but also, don't let me waste away with a dulled passion, a limited hope, and an empty life."

So far, God has answered those prayers.

CONSIDER THIS

Is Jesus beautiful to you? How can you tell?

What do your deepest desires, the ones you ponder when no one else is around, tell you about your heart? What pursuits make you feel alive, and which ones deaden you?

Are you being vilified for loving people who are outside your tribe? If so, how are you handling it? If not, what needs to change?

What does it look like to be fully abandoned to God in a self-indulgent culture?

Chapter 10

THE NEGLECTED SOURCE

From Pragmatics to Supernatural Power

I sometimes hear American pastors say, "Yes, I believe in the ministry of the Holy Spirit, but I'm cautious about it." Can you imagine someone sharing the gospel and telling an unbeliever, "You need to receive Christ, but you need to be cautious about your commitment"? We'd never say that!

The Holy Spirit isn't the junior member of the Trinity, but he is the member of the Godhead who makes us uncomfortable, or as one person wryly described him, he's "the weird uncle." The Spirit of God is the source of everything beautiful and wonderful in our lives. Among many other ways he impacts our lives, the Holy Spirit is an agent of creation, draws sinners to Christ, illumes the Scriptures so we understand God's truth, assures us we belong to God, guides us, convicts us and assures us of forgiveness, anoints us with divine power, is our advocate, bestows spiritual gifts, and produces spiritual fruit in us. A few years ago, the trucking industry put an ad on television that said, "If you've got it, a truck brought it." We could very accurately say, "If you've got anything good and right and lovely in your life, the Holy Spirit brought it."

Instead of being cautious about him, we need to abandon ourselves to him just as much as we abandon ourselves to the Father and the Son. Instead, too many of us have limited the Spirit of God, putting him in a box of reservations and doubts, limiting his role in our lives and ministries. Don't get me wrong. I understand there are plenty of bizarre things people ascribe to the Holy Spirit, but don't we have the wisdom to distinguish between the bizarre and the beautiful, the manipulative and the mighty? Of course we do.

Many of us want to have every detail of theology about the Spirit nailed down, for ourselves and the people in our churches, before we're willing to trust him to do magnificent things in us and through us. What a lack of faith! We've tried to reduce him to a manageable size, but he's infinite, beyond our comprehension. We'll never have him fully figured out or under our control, and he invites us to trust him and experience his presence and power.

I've talked to American Christians—especially pastors—who are terrified of what the Holy Spirit will do if they fully yield themselves to him. They don't need to be afraid. He loves them more than they can ever imagine and has more wisdom than they'll ever grasp.

In the rest of the world, the Pentecostal movement is growing more rapidly than any other segment of the Christian world. The global pastors I know aren't scared of the Holy Spirit. They read the Bible, recognize the clear teaching about the roles of the Spirit, and trust him to do what only he can do. But in their parts of the world, they've also observed the same excesses many American pastors fear. Eddy Leo calls some of the purveyors of strange teaching and behavior "charismaniacs." Eddy believes in the power of the Spirit and all the gifts of the Spirit, but he's not a charismaniac.

Throughout the world, and even in East Texas where I grew up, the charismatic movement has made great strides in the last four or five decades. In the '70s, my father was a Baptist pastor in Lindale, Texas. The little town buzzed when David Wilkerson, the author of *The Cross and the Switchblade*, moved into our community. We expected him to attend the local Pentecostal church so he'd feel comfortable with sawdust, snakes, and people being slain in the Spirit. (At least, that's what we assumed happened there.) But the next Sunday, he showed up at my dad's church. Soon, he brought a bunch of teenagers to our church. A week or so later, he asked my father to meet with him. Dad wasn't sure what the conversation was going to be about. Would Wilkerson try to change his theology and practice? It was nothing like that at all. When they met, Wilkerson thanked my dad for his leadership, and he said, "I can teach these kids what I want them to know about the Holy Spirit, but they need your teaching to ground them in the Word of God." My dad was blown away by Wilkerson's humility and kindness. He wasn't weird at all!

Eventually, a number of other charismatic leaders attended our church. They didn't feel judged by my dad, and they appreciated his teaching. And I made a startling discovery: they loved God as much or more than I did, and they served him with at least as much passion as I had. Because of them, my harsh stereotypes of Pentecostals began to erode.

When I was fourteen, I heard a pastor talk about giving up our rights and putting our lives in the loving, strong hands of God. His message hit me like a brick truck. For the first time in my life, I sensed the presence of the Spirit and his unmistakable prompting. With a clear mind and an open heart, I gave up my right to define my future, my right to decide who I would marry, my right to a comfortable life, and my right to fulfill my own dreams. I told God that I was an empty vessel, and I invited him to fill it. For several hours, the Holy Spirit fell on me. He was more real than I'd ever sensed before.

But this experience was outside the box of our Baptist theology and experiences—or at least I thought it was. I deeply appreciated what God had done in that special time to meet with me and fill my heart with his presence and power, but I was confused about what to do next. All around us, churches were splitting over the role of the Spirit. Was I going to become an outcast? Was I becoming weird?

It took years for me to put this experience in an understandable context. I didn't learn this context from seminary or from being a pastor; I learned it from my friends who are pastors around the world.

TURNING POINT

By 1988, I'd become a fan and follower of Rick Warren, and he and I began developing a relationship. He was invited to speak to a gathering of pastors in Tanzania and Kenya, but at the last minute, something came up and he couldn't go. To my surprise, he called me and said, "Bob, if you'll go to speak to these pastors, your way is completely paid." I was just a pup. Who was I to stand in for Rick Warren? But I couldn't pass up the opportunity.

When I arrived at the pastors' conference, I got very sick. In the afternoon before my talk scheduled for the first night, I was in so much pain that I could barely stand up. I was sweating profusely, and my chest felt like someone had stuck an ice pick in it. The people there thought I was having a heart attack.

The conference director asked a Dutch doctor to look at me. He examined me and announced, "I think you have kidney stones. We need to take you to a hospital."

I didn't want to leave the event, but the pain was so severe there was no way I could stand and speak, even for a few minutes. I was completely debilitated. The conference director conferred with some other leaders and told me, "We have a Baptist Pentecostal pastor who can pray for you. Do you want me to ask him to come in?"

I moaned, "It can't hurt."

A few minutes later, Joseph Maisha walked into the room. It was the first time we had ever met. He laid his hands on me and prayed. Almost immediately, I went into a deep sleep.

All afternoon, the director worked to arrange a flight for me to go to Nairobi and then back to the States. At six that evening, I woke up. I felt no pain at all. I began to sit up, but a man who had been in the room watching me all afternoon quickly told me, "Bob, don't move. If it's a kidney stone, you might dislodge it and the pain will come back."

As I lay there, I thought, *That pastor asked God to heal me, and maybe—just maybe—he did. I don't believe God brought me all the way to East Africa to get sick and have to fly home. I believe he wants me to serve these pastors.* Then the thought hit me, *This illness is from Satan because he doesn't want me to share all I've learned from Rick Warren and John Maxwell.*

Again, I started to sit up, and again, the man in my room told me to be still. This time I responded, "I appreciate your concern, but I believe God wants me to speak to the pastors at this conference. I'm going to do it."

I spoke many times over the next three days, all without a hint of pain. When it was over, the director flew me to Nairobi to see a doctor. After he used a dye to look at an X-ray of my kidneys, he asked, "When did you pass the kidney stone?"

I answered, "I didn't."

He looked puzzled, pointed to the X-ray, and said, "Do you see all this damage? It's from a very large kidney stone. There's no way you could have passed it without excruciating pain … and without knowing it came out."

This was my first personal encounter with miraculous healing. For months after my trip to Tanzania and Kenya, I tried to find Joseph to thank him, but I was unsuccessful. A few years later, Shadrach, a Kenyan pastor in the Dallas–Fort Worth area, was listening to a pastor give a talk on engaging the city, and he thought, *That man sounds like Bob Roberts!* Shadrach and I had known each other, but we hadn't connected for some time. He called me and said he wanted me to meet one of his friends. He brought his friend to my house, and I knew immediately: it was Joseph! It was a glorious reunion! I discovered that Joseph was a Baptist who believed in the power of the Holy Spirit. In his church in Mombasa, his ministry delivers people from demons and heals sickness by the power of the Spirit. He believes in miracles, and God performs miracles. He has been a part of the collaborative gathering of pastors for many years now.

Outside the borders of America, the vast majority of pastors and church leaders believe in the Spirit's presence, purpose, and power to do far more than the typical American can imagine. As I've rubbed shoulders with my new friends from around the world, I've learned much more about the Holy Spirit and experienced more of his reality.

One of the biggest lessons I've learned is that we should follow the Holy Spirit. We follow the example of Jesus and his teachings, but day by day and moment by moment in all situations, we must learn to recognize the Spirit at work and follow him. I had been so busy trying to find the "biblical" view of the Holy Spirit that I didn't know the Holy Spirit as a person and I didn't understand how the Holy Spirit worked. I also realized it's easy to get out of balance in our understanding of the Holy Spirit. Pastors from my background often ignore scriptures about the Holy Spirit, and charismatics and Pentecostals sometimes add teaching, assumptions, and practices beyond what the Bible says about the Spirit.

I also began to see a crucial truth about the Christian life: without the love, power, and presence of the Holy Spirit, I could never live the Sermon on the Mount. All my attempts to live a righteous life were doomed to failure, unless I experienced the love, forgiveness, and power of the Spirit. And without the Holy Spirit, we can never fulfill the Great Commission. As I began to study the scriptures relating to the Spirit, I realized the gifts of the Spirit weren't given to make me successful, but to bring glory to God and to touch the lives of others. Without the Holy Spirit operating powerfully in my motives, desires, and actions, life was all about me. But with the Spirit of God making the love and strength of God real to me, his power could work in me and then through me. I could fulfill my calling only as the Holy Spirit was free to have his way in me.

WRONG QUESTIONS, RIGHT QUESTIONS

In the 1880s, many of the leading pastors and theologians in the West—including D. L. Moody, Andrew Murray, Charles Spurgeon, and R. A. Torrey—taught clearly and powerfully about the Holy Spirit and sometimes had "tarrying meetings" for people to experience the fullness of the Spirit. After Azusa Street in 1906, however, things changed. To avoid being painted with the same brush, many Christian leaders started drawing hard lines to create boundaries of teaching and experience. Since then, many of us have asked the wrong questions.

Wrong question: *When* are you filled with the Holy Spirit?
Right question: *Have you* been filled with the Holy Spirit?

Our experience with the reality of God isn't flipping a switch or having some kind of triggered emotional moment. It's a relationship, one we enter and develop over time. The marks of a relationship between two people are love, understanding, empathy, and support—which are exactly (but only part of) the attributes of our relationship with God when we let the Spirit have his way in us.

Also, being filled isn't an episodic series of spectacular events. The relationship begins and deepens as we love and trust God more. We are "continually being filled" with the Spirit. The Azusa Street experiences took the focus off the relationship and put it on a moment when people experienced a dramatic, ecstatic encounter with God. It's more than that. It's a vital love connection with God.

If you're not sure if you're filled, ask him to fill you. Jesus assures us:

> For everyone who asks receives, and the one who seeks finds, and to the one who knocks it will be opened. What father among you, if his son asks for a fish, will instead of a fish give him a serpent; or if he asks for an egg, will give him a scorpion? If you then, who are evil, know how to give good gifts to your children, how much more will the heavenly Father give the Holy Spirit to those who ask him! (Luke 11:10–13)

Wrong question: Have you *spoken in tongues*?
Right question: Are you *being transformed*?

Many of my Pentecostal friends assert that speaking in tongues is "initial physical evidence" of the filling of the Spirit, just as it was at Pentecost for the believers in the Upper Room. But I've known some wonderful believers who have grown up in Pentecostal churches but have never spoken in tongues, and I know some Christians in traditionally noncharismatic churches who speak in tongues. I don't think that's the main issue. When the Spirit of God captures our hearts and reveals his greatness and grace, he changes us from the inside out. A sure sign of the Spirit is the increasing growth of spiritual fruit (Gal. 5:22–23). We don't just conform to outward rules or expectations; we increasingly *want* to obey God, we *want* to pray to get near him, we *want* to love the unlovely, and we *want* to reflect his kindness, justice, and righteousness.

Wrong question: What *is* my spiritual gift?
Right question: What *are* my spiritual gifts?

I think many Western believers are too narrow about the Bible's teaching about the gifts of the Spirit. We find lists in Ephesians 4, 1 Peter 4, Romans 12, and 1 Corinthians 12, but they aren't the same. Did Paul and Peter need an editor? No, they were providing a few representative gifts in each list for their readers. We can conclude, then, that God is far more creative and far more flexible than our inventories and lists. God empowers each of us to meet particular needs. In his great wisdom and love, he puts us where he wants us at any given moment and equips us for the task. I don't believe God is stingy in giving us gifts; he's generous to pour out his power into and through us.

Every gift is available to every believer to accomplish the purposes of God. He chooses to call us, use us, and empower us to accomplish his purposes. This means we don't boast about our gifts and we don't feel resentful that someone has a gift we don't have. It's all about God's calling, God's kingdom, and God's glory. We should never limit God as he works in our lives.

Wrong question: What does the Spirit do *for me*?
Right question: What does the Spirit do *for us*?

Too often we've made the teaching about spiritual gifts all about our ability to shine, but the gifts aren't given for that purpose. The Spirit bestows these special abilities to advance the kingdom and build up Christ's body. It's about us, not me. We use the gifts to serve and bless others, not to impress people.

After he gave a short list of the gifted roles of leaders for the church, Paul explained, "Rather, speaking the truth in love, we are to grow up in every way into him who is the head, into Christ, from whom the whole body, joined and held together by every joint with which it is equipped, when each part is working properly, makes the body grow so that it builds itself up in love" (Eph. 4:15–16).

Wrong question: What does the Holy Spirit do *in me*?
Right question: What does the Holy Spirit do *through me*?

Yes, thank God, the Spirit works *in us* to transform us, but that's not the end of the story. God's purpose isn't for us to feel good about ourselves, but to invest our lives in his kingdom so that others will know and love him—like Abraham, to be blessed so we'll be a blessing. The Spirit isn't our personal power source; he's the source of a life of love and power that overflows into the lives of everyone we touch. In a self-absorbed, self-indulgent world, it's easy to think of the Spirit's power as a personal possession. But he has bigger plans than that.

We also make another error. We assume the benchmark of the Spirit's presence is signs and wonders, but it's far more miraculous for men and women to be so transformed that they live the Sermon on the Mount in front of their families, friends, and coworkers.

Wrong question: What do I say *no* to?
Right question: What do I say *yes* to?

Some conscientious Christians are more obsessed with rules than their relationship with God. Certainly, the Bible contains warnings and directives that are given to prevent us from messing up our lives. We're not antinomian, but the rules don't give spiritual life. One of the most important factors in my spiritual life is that I've been learning to listen to the voice of God and respond with glad obedience. Two truths beautifully blend to give me direction and assurance: God is the sovereign ruler over all things, and the Holy Spirit orchestrates our lives to lead us where he wants us to go and empowers us to fulfill his purposes. As the Spirit changes our desires, we increasingly pray, "Your kingdom come." We want God to be honored more than we want personal applause, and we want God's power to be demonstrated more than we want control of people and situations. And we pray, "Your will be done on earth as it is in heaven." We are open and available to the opportunities the Spirit brings into our day.

When interruptions happened, I used to get upset. Now I'm beginning to look for the Holy Spirit in them. Maybe he's opening a door to love someone, to show his grace, or to speak the truth. I can say yes to him at every moment.

Wrong question: What do I *do*?
Right question: What do I *hear*?

Most pastors in the West are focused on accomplishing our plans and keeping our schedules. We're all about accomplishment—and we define what qualifies as our accomplishments. In contrast, the pastors in the Global Collaborative Community are amazingly open to the Lord's whispers, promptings, and nudgings. They believe they have a vital relationship with God, not something stiff, distant, or stale. And they expect him to break in to redirect them at any point in the day. It's so refreshing to be with them!

Many of us in the West want to have all our ducks in a row before we take any risks for God. But I've noticed that God often withholds the abundance of his wisdom and power until we've acted on the leading he has already given us. We want everything in place before we step out, but that's not a life of faith, and that's not how the Spirit works.

Wrong question: What is *my dream*?

Right question: How can I *glorify God*?

In his book *New Rules*, Daniel Yankelovich observed that in the decade of the 1950s, our culture moved from *self-sacrifice* before and during World War II to *self-indulgence*.[1] Do you think Western pastors have been affected by this change? Of course we have. The expectation that God exists to fulfill our dreams is woven throughout the fabric of our culture, including the church. One of the sure signs that the Holy Spirit is at work is the convicting realization that our dreams of success matter more to us than God's kingdom. We've worried more about our reputations than God's glory. We've been happier about the growth of our churches than the growth of the global church.

The Bible says that all of us boast about something (Jer. 9:23–24; 1 Cor. 1:31; Gal. 6:14). As the Spirit works in the heart of those of us who live in a self-indulgent world, we begin to boast about God's love, his power, and the wonder of his grace more than we boast about our achievements, fame, and talents.

Wrong question: Where am I going in *the future*?
Right question: What is God doing in *this moment*?

Learning to live in the present has been one of the most revolutionary changes God has made in my life. For years, I lived in the future. I either daydreamed about accomplishing great things or worried I wouldn't. When situations or people interrupted my day, I was frustrated because they took me away from my heart's misguided purpose. As I've learned to listen to the Spirit of God, however, things have changed. I realize that each moment is a gift from God, and I need to listen to him each moment. I still miss a lot of "God moments" when I'm preoccupied with my agenda and plans, but not as many as before. And quite often—more often than I ever imagined—God breaks into my day to give me opportunities to be his hands, feet, and voice to care for people I may have overlooked in the past.

Wrong question: What are *people* telling me?
Right question: What is *the Spirit* telling me?

For years, I sought the counsel of mentors, friends, and scholars, but I seldom, if ever, expected God's Spirit to break in and give me directions. The Bible tells us to listen to wise people, but it's not either/or. Today, I'm learning to listen to the Spirit first and then talk to others to get their opinions. Quite often they affirm what I've heard the Spirit say to me, but sometimes I get conflicting advice. When this happens, I ask my friends to pray with me so we both hear from God. That usually solves the problem.

We prepare our hearts to hear God by having regular times of Bible study and prayer, soaking our minds and hearts in the truth of his greatness and grace, understanding his purposes more fully, and inviting him to have his way in us. If we're listening to him during these focused times, we'll be more likely to hear him throughout the rest of our day.

As we learn to ask the right questions, we realize our utter helplessness apart from God's Spirit. In much of the American church, we don't think we need the Holy Spirit. If we have our demographic and psychographic study of our community, develop a strategic plan, create great marketing, and write a sharp mission statement, we're ready to go. But if we trust in the Spirit of God, we no longer rely on our slick marketing, our seminary degrees, or the tips we've learned from the latest conferences. I'm not demeaning the value of these things, but they must not be our primary source of power and wisdom.

As I've spent time with the pastors from around the world, I've realized there's a spiritual world far more wonderful yet far more sinister than I'd believed. Three times in Paul's letter to the Ephesians, he said that Christ's power was greater than "all rule and authority and power and dominion" (Eph. 1:21; see also 3:10; 6:12), the powers we can see and the powers we can't see. In India, pastor Joshua Vjaykumar sees the power of evil spirits when Christians share the good news about Christ. He explained, "Very often, when we hold a gospel meeting, a demon-possessed person comes to the front of our meeting and dances. This is a direct challenge to God's authority in front of all the people. We have to drive off the evil spirit immediately. Unless people realize the power of the Holy Spirit, they will not understand that our God is more powerful than the evil spirits."

The seen and the unseen often collide in times of famine, opposition, and sickness. In the West, we're insulated from desperation, but not in the East. A pastor in Southeast Asia once told me, "Bob, we have Jeremiah 33:3; you have doctors. We don't have the luxury of not trusting God. He's all we've got. When people around you are dying of hunger, when your life is threatened because you're sharing the gospel, and when your child is sick and there are no doctors, the Holy Spirit isn't a nice addition to your life—he's essential."

BE OPEN

My Pentecostal and charismatic friends reading this chapter are smiling and saying, "Bob, what took you so long?" And some are asking, "But, Bob, have you really experienced the fullness of the Spirit?" But those who aren't in that camp are probably guarded. They've heard the stories about the crazy things people claim the Holy Spirit has done in individuals and churches, and they want no part of that! I'm not recommending anything bizarre. Just be open to the wonder of the Spirit's presence in your life. Don't be so cautious. Don't try to speak in tongues, and don't try to avoid tongues. Just pray, "God, I'm opening my life to your Spirit. I'm not putting any limitations on you. Do in me and through me whatever you will. I'm yours."

Then, be yourself. Read your Bible and pray, and serve God in your community and your church; but expect the Spirit to break in. Listen more closely, and look for signs of him at work. Expect more and notice more. You'll see more of the Holy Spirit's presence all around you. As you align your heart and your life with him, he'll give you all the gifts you need to fulfill his purposes. When our lives are in lockstep with the mission and ministry of God's kingdom, God pours out his resources on us. He doesn't give them ahead of time—he gives them in the moment we need to use them.

Most of the time, the Spirit shows up in ways that are gentle and kind, but sometimes, it's dramatic. When I was in a part of the world where Christians aren't honored and are often persecuted, I met with a number of leaders of the country. As I prayed in my room before the meeting, the word "blood" came to mind. I dismissed it and went to the meeting. That night, the word came to me again. I prayed, "God, this is kind of strange. I don't know what 'blood' means. Are you trying to tell me something?" No answer came.

The next day during the meeting, the word "blood" kept coming to mind. At a break, I was talking to one of the leaders when another powerful man walked by. When he was out of hearing range, the man talking to me leaned over and whispered, "Bob, you need to be very careful around that man. He's the bloodiest man in this country. He savagely kills his opponents."

Instantly, I understood. The Spirit of God had been warning me to be circumspect around that particular man. You can call it a word of knowledge or you can call it something else. All I know is that the Holy Spirit had my back!

At another event, I was asked to speak to a group of world leaders on the impact of the Great Commission on a culture when commit-ted disciples engage their culture. I explained that Christians who are sharing the love of God and living the Sermon on the Mount are a blessing to every society because they spread kindness, integrity, wisdom, and justice. Those who have been forgiven can display forgiveness, and those who have been reconciled to God and to others can offer the process of reconciliation between races, religions, and nations. Sounds like a pretty good message, doesn't it? Actually, the Spirit gave me that message just before I got up to speak. I hadn't planned to talk on that topic at all. The concepts came to mind as clearly as if I were reading them from a script. Until that day, I'd been a bit skeptical of the promise that the Holy Spirit would bring things to mind when we need them, but since that day, I've been a believer.

If we're open to the Spirit, some amazing things might happen. A couple of years ago, I met an ayatollah. I told him if he ever wanted to visit our church, I'd love to host him. He called a few weeks later and said he would like to come for Easter! He flew to the Dallas–Fort Worth Airport, and we had him over to our house on Friday night and Saturday. On Sunday morning, he came to our packed service wearing his full robes and turban. During the service, I asked him if he'd like us to pray for him. He said, "I would be honored." Before I began praying, our teenagers came forward to gather around him. They prayed for peace between our two countries.

I was surprised when I saw one of the young men who reached out to touch the ayatollah when they prayed. I didn't even know he was a Christian. Later, he told me he had recently trusted Christ. He said, "If God can save me, he can save an ayatollah."

A week later, President Obama announced the beginning of negotiations with the leaders of Iran to stop the construction of a nuclear bomb and begin to resolve the long-standing differences between our two countries. The students in our church saw this as an answer to their prayers. A few months later, this ayatollah invited me to travel to Iran to meet with other leaders of his country. God was, indeed, opening doors.

I've been learning to recognize divine moments, and I've also discovered that seemingly insignificant moments, especially with seemingly insignificant people, are often vitally important to God. These were the people Jesus delighted to love. The principle is clear: to the degree we are abandoned to God and open to his purpose, we'll have the joy of experiencing the presence and power of the Holy Spirit. I don't believe the manifestation of the reality of the Spirit comes until we're in line with God's mission. Some of my charismatic friends would say that you have to get free of sin's grip first, but this freedom is the first step in God's mission in us so that he can work through us.

As you consider the role of the Holy Spirit in your life, here's my advice:

- As you study and read each morning, pray, "Holy Spirit, speak to me."
- When you're meeting with people in the community, pray, "Give me eyes to see what you want me to see in people's lives. Don't let me ignore people I might overlook."
- In every conversation, be sensitive to the Spirit's whispers and nudges. Don't assume you know what's going on. There's a universe of spiritual forces at work, in addition to the hidden motives of every person's heart.

- Don't wait for the big events and big challenges to look for the Spirit. He's in the little moments too.

But understand this: following the Spirit doesn't necessarily mean your dreams will come true, but you can be assured that you'll be in alignment with God's kingdom values.

If you're not from a charismatic background, make friends with a charismatic or two. You don't have to agree on every point of theology to learn from each other. Let your friend's openness to the Spirit push you a little bit.

CONSIDER THIS

As I meet with pastors across America, I'm struck by the fact that many of them have a deep, nagging sense that they need more of God. They're filled with unmet needs and unanswered questions. They know there's more, but they don't know where to go to find the solution. They want to experience more depth and richness in their relationship with God, but they don't want to be one of those crazy Pentecostals. It's a false choice.

If that's you, open your heart to God. Ask him to fill you with the Holy Spirit. He's not weird. The Holy Spirit is the Spirit of Jesus. Look in the Gospels at Christ's kindness and courage. That's exactly how the Holy Spirit wants to relate to you and work through you.

But remember: It's not just about you and your gifts and fruitfulness. God wants to use you to have an impact on your city and the world. Without the very real power and wisdom of the Spirit, you're not firing on all cylinders. You have more power available if you're open to receiving it!

Don't forget about God after you close your Bible from preparing for your sermon or having your devotions. Live with God in the moment, every moment. Sometimes the Spirit will break in to change your plans. Let him do it. Listen and obey. Learn great spiritual lessons from Jesus, who told us to pay attention to the Spirit when he comes. He's come! Pay attention to him.

Don't be afraid of getting it wrong. I assure you, you will. Sometimes you'll think the Holy Spirit's whisper is just indigestion, and sometimes you'll think he gave you clear direction but your attempt to follow him bombed. Don't worry about it. You're learning, you're growing, and you'll improve in your sensitivity to him.

Take a minute to stop right now and pray, "Holy Spirit, I want you to have all of me, and I want all of you. I want to walk in another dimension. Teach me, fill me, use me."

Chapter 11

PRAYER

From Expendable to Essential

When I meet with the pastors in our Global Collaborative Community, the first thing we do is get on our knees and pray—and these guys know how to pray! We often pray for long periods, lifting up praises to God for who he is and all he's done and pleading with God to do mighty things in us and through us. The needs in the lives of these men aren't for a parking spot near the door at the mall. They bring concerns that would stagger many of us in America: death threats from terrorists, government oppression, demonic powers, and life-threatening sickness without modern medical care. They ask God to put his heart for the lost and the least into the hearts of their people back home. They ask him to open doors in the public square with top leaders and in every corner of their communities so their people can serve as lights of Christ.

I took a very successful American executive with me to one of our gatherings in Korea. I was more than a little apprehensive about his reaction to the first hour or two in prayer. These times aren't like the normal Wednesday night prayer services at a Baptist church. These men shout their praises and weep their hurts.

After a long while, I looked over at the executive. He was sobbing. When I approached him, his eyes were as wide as a five-year-old at Disneyland. He said, "Bob, I've been a Christian for many years, but I've never experienced anything like this." He must have thought about all I'd told him concerning my times with these leaders. He paused for a second, and then he told me, "I get it now. I really get it. There's something different about these guys." He paused for a second and then said, "I can see why you want to spend time with them."

The pastors hadn't talked about goals or strategies or stories of God's love and power. He had just met these men, and we had only prayed, but it was enough to show him that these men had something he'd never encountered before.

KINGDOM PRAYERS

When God opened my eyes to the kingdom, my prayer life changed radically. Several things happened simultaneously: I began to hear the voice of God as a normal part of my relationship with him, I started seeing that the cause of Christ was far bigger than the walls of our church or the shores of our nation, and I discovered I was a phenomenal Baptist but a lousy follower of Jesus. I could follow rules with the best of them, but I couldn't live the Sermon on the Mount without the fullness of the indwelling Spirit of God. I became so desperate to know God and experience his presence and power that I determined to be more focused. For me, being more focused meant writing my thoughts and prayers as I read the Bible. My devotional life moved from merely reading and reflecting to genuine encounters with the living God.

In my office I have a stack of journals I've filled over the years, and I treasure them. When I meet with God, I pour out my heart to him. I tell him how much I love him, and I try to describe his indescribable wonders. I tell him what I'm worried about and what I want from him. And I tell him I'm open to hear anything he wants to say to me. I ask him for wisdom to face the challenges of the day. When I read the Bible, I pray, "Holy Spirit, speak to me through your Word." And he does.

Before this change, I often got distracted when I prayed, and I found it hard to spend more than fifteen minutes in prayer. Suddenly, I couldn't get enough of God! I delighted in him, and I sensed his delight in me. Who would want to rush that? Now when I sense God saying something to me, I write it down. Sometimes I don't even get to petitions because I'm "lost in wonder, love and praise." I don't think he minds.

As I got to know the men in our global community, I discovered all of them have rich, real prayer lives. They don't see prayer as merely a duty to perform. Like all of us, sometimes they don't want to pray, and they pray only out of obedience, but most of the time they delight in communing with the matchless God of power and grace.

DIVIDING LINES

A LifeWay survey found that almost half of all Americans, 48 percent, pray daily, and 37 percent say God answers their prayers "some of the time."[1] The West has a long history of making prayer a priority.

In recent years, Philip Yancey, J. I. Packer, and Tim Keller have written excellent books on prayer. These works and the teaching of many pastors point us to prayer as the source of comfort, strength, and direction. In the American church, however, we often emphasize two secondary things: prayer methodology and prayer gatherings. The pastors from the other side of the world have a different emphasis: prayer as a lifestyle and a lifeline. Communicating with God to draw on his wisdom and power isn't an occasional event; it's woven into the fabric of their daily lives—in every event, every conversation, every blessing, and every challenge. For them, prayer is designed to accomplish eight purposes:

- They worship God.
- They find a source of power to do kingdom work.
- They experience freedom from their limitations.
- They intercede for their movements.
- They need wisdom for the cataclysmic decisions regarding the lives of people they love.
- They draw on God's power to wrestle with demonic forces.
- They're expecting revelations from God.
- They get directives from God before they take action.

Among many pastors I know in our country, we often pray so God will make our lives comfortable, we pray to be more successful in comparison to our peers, and we pray because we hope God will make us nice people. In other cultures, pastors and all Christians lean into God so they can survive another day and bring the kingdom of God into reality in their communities. For us, we often tack on a prayer for guidance after we've read books, made a pro-con list, and talked to others to get their advice. For them, prayer is the first priority and source of wisdom to know how to live for God each moment of the day.

When my global friends pray, they redefine the meaning of the word "fervent." They're passionate about God and his purposes. They weep and wail and shout as they communicate with God.

They invest significant time in prayer, often beginning early in the morning and continuing throughout the day. They never seem to be in a hurry, and prayer never seems perfunctory.

They pray with a strong sense of expectancy. They don't just hope God will answer; God *has to* answer or they're in big trouble!

Their prayers are amazingly interactive. They stop to listen to the whispers and shouts of the Spirit. They pull out their Bibles to read a passage to direct their prayers. And they often stop to talk to one another to ask, "What are you hearing from God as we pray?"

They lay hold of the promises of God and pray with authority. They say, "Lord, I come as your child to the throne of grace, and I ask, not in my name, but in the name of Jesus." They may pray, "God, if you don't come through, the people will laugh at you," or "Lord, you told me to do this for you, and I'm counting on you to provide."

These pastors don't get hung up on theological disputes between God's sovereignty and man's choices. Terry Virgo commented, "I enjoy the fullness of the Holy Spirit, but I'm always subject to the authority of Scripture. The apostle Paul was full of the Holy Spirit and wrote Romans, perhaps the greatest theological treatise ever penned. He taught us about the sovereignty of God, but he encouraged us in Ephesians to address one another in psalms and hymns and spiritual songs, singing and making melody to the Lord with your heart. To him, there was no conflict between heartfelt love, exuberant praise and thanksgiving, and the absolute rule of God. He didn't take sides, and neither should we. Sometimes when I go to conferences, they ask me to check a box, either Reformed or charismatic. I check both."

Their prayers are punctuated with transparency and confession. As they praise God for the wonders of his power and sovereignty, they become increasingly aware of their smallness and sins. But in this, they're assured of God's wonderful power and forgiveness. They're vulnerable with each other. If they sense doubt or fear, or perhaps some demonic oppression, they tell others and ask them to pray for faith and freedom.

Most American pastors have a wealth of resources: education, strategies, conferences, books, and seminars. The global pastors have far fewer resources; they only have God, the Scriptures, and each other. From what I've seen in our country, prayer is too organized, too formulaic, and too bland. Of course, many of our Pentecostal brothers and sisters break this pattern, but the rest of us in America could learn some things from the pastors on the other side of the world. They aren't very organized; they're open to whatever God wants to do in the moment. They don't follow formulas for prayer, but they have power and passion. They don't see prayer as a Christian activity to perform; they see it as an opportunity to spend time with their Father, the mighty, loving king. We get caught up with techniques, but they delight in their identity as chosen, forgiven, adopted, beloved, empowered children of God.

A BIGGER VISION, BIGGER PRAYER

If a pastor is trying to build his church, and he believes Sunday morning is the most important hour of the week, his prayers will be focused on asking God to make the worship service as attractive as possible and finding enough volunteers to pull it off. But if he is engaging leaders in the public square, serving faithfully and creatively in the domains of the community, planting churches in the city, and making a difference in other parts of the world, he'll be far more desperate for God to show up and do what only God can do. Ministry techniques don't matter very much. Also, the needs of his church won't matter as much because his eyes will be fixed on a far bigger goal: building the kingdom of God by serving the city and going to the world.

When we have a bigger vision, we don't pray and check it off as a duty we've performed. We pray because our hearts are captured by the glory of God, the mission of the kingdom, and the fact that only the Spirit can change lives. We long for people—the high and the low, the Republicans and the Democrats, Americans and Asians and Africans and all the rest—to experience the wonder of God's grace and glory.

If we, like the apostle Paul, engage the public square, two important things happen: we become more deeply aware of our need for God to give us wisdom and strength, and all our people who serve in their domains don't lose contact with unbelievers. Studies show that most new Christians no longer have meaningful contact with their unbelieving friends after a year or two. However, when Christians are involved in schools, markets, government, medicine, the arts, and all the other domains, they maintain contact with lost people, love them, and see more of them come to Christ. They'll have more reasons to pray because they stay connected to unbelievers.

When we have a kingdom perspective, our prayers for ourselves change. We no longer focus on what we want to make us happy and more successful. As we rub shoulders with people in domains and are exposed to their needs, we may become aware of our hardness of heart—and it's no longer acceptable. In the last few years as God has led me to meet with leaders all over the world, I've seen traits in me that I've excused or ignored all my life. I realized I can be intense, aggressive, and demanding, so I asked God to give me the gift of gentleness. I grew up working hard in the fields of East Texas. I worked summers in a foundry and a pipe factory. I often came home black from head to toe with grease and oil. These are places where gentleness and kindness aren't valued in men. We were expected to work hard, kill animals, and overhaul engines.

The concept of a "gentleman" isn't a sissy. It's a strong, mature, accomplished man who knows how to handle every situation with skill and tact. In my conversations with national and global leaders, and in my relationships with my spiritual sons, I need to be a gentleman, not a bull. Paul instructed the Colossians:

> Put on then, as God's chosen ones, holy and
> beloved, compassionate hearts, kindness, humility,
> meekness, and patience, bearing with one another

> and, if one has a complaint against another, for-
> giving each other; as the Lord has forgiven you, so
> you also must forgive. And above all these put on
> love, which binds everything together in perfect
> harmony. (Col. 3:12–14)

These traits aren't about being powerful and persuasive. They're all about gentleness. I'm encouraged that Paul didn't say, "Some of you are temperamentally kind, and the rest of you have no hope of ever being tender and gracious." Instead, he pointed them to their identity in Christ, as God's chosen and beloved, as the hope for real change. As we experience God's kindness, we become kinder. As we marvel at his patience, we become more patient. As we realize Jesus humbled himself to leave the glory of heaven to die a horrible death for us, we won't be as cocky. As we receive the gift of grace more fully each day, we'll become givers instead of takers.

When God began to put the prayer for gentleness on my heart, I stood in front of our church and confessed, "You know I'm not gentle. That's not good. It's not like Jesus, but God wants to do some-thing in me. Please pray for me."

The kindest, gentlest man I've ever known was C. U. Callahan. I'm getting older, and I want to follow his example as I get nearer to the finish line. In the '20s, he became an orphan when his parents were killed in a car wreck. He went to live with his aunt, who didn't provide much love for him. During World War II, he became a tank com-mander. He was the consummate tough guy, but with a tender heart. He became a Christian when he was older, and he joined my dad's church. Our church and our family were very poor, but C. U. had some money—and he was generous. There were many Christmases when I was a boy when there would have been no presents if it hadn't been for C. U. I grew up thinking he was part of our family. He wasn't, but it didn't matter. He was so kind, gentle, and tender. He had a ready smile and a forgiving heart. He was a terrific role model for me, but for most of my adult life, I didn't follow his example. I'm not saying I've been abusive, but I could have been a lot gentler to the people around me. In the last few years, I've reflected more often on the loving look in C. U.'s eyes and the kindness of his heart. I want to be more like him.

God is working on me. Not long ago, my son came home and asked my wife, "What's going on with Dad? He's a lot softer than he used to be."

And my wife told me, "Bob, you're different. God is answering my prayers!" I'm so grateful. I'm not where I need to be, but thank God, I'm not where I was. Indeed, God has been answering our prayers.

In our prayers of confession, we often focus on the most obvious sins, but we frequently fail to notice the selfish motives under a lot of our behavior, even our "good and right" behavior. God is as interested in our motives as he is in our actions, maybe more. Many people today blame their bad behavior on their parents. Certainly, difficult backgrounds can wound us and distort our views in many ways, but it's time to take responsibility for our lives. No more blame shifting; no more excusing or minimizing. We need to own our selfish thoughts, words, and actions, as well as our motives, and be honest with God about them. Honest prayer leads us to experience God's forgiveness, and then we can forgive those who hurt us out of the deep well of our experience of God's grace. If prayer doesn't take us into a deeper grasp of our sin and a deeper experience of God's grace, we're missing something.

STRENGTH WHEN WE NEED IT

For the pastors in the Global Collaborative Community, prayer helps them reinterpret opposition, heartache, and suffering. They don't crater when things don't go the way they hoped. They *expect* attacks, setbacks, and hardships of all kinds, and they pour out their hearts to the Lord. Just across our border with Mexico, conflict between the drug cartels and the government has cost tens of thousands of lives. In the power struggle, some pastors are caught in the crosshairs. Pablo is a church planter in that troubled land. He reported, "Some cities are in the hands of the cartels, and they are kidnapping pastors who stand up to them. A pastor in our organization was kidnapped two years ago, and we don't even know if he is still alive. Another pastor was kidnapped recently. The cartel beat him badly and demanded a ransom, but he escaped. These are not isolated instances. They are more common than you know."

Pablo asked a friend who is a pastor in Colombia for advice. His friend, who had seen similar violence in his country, told him, "Be humble and wise. We all are committed to stand up for Jesus, but there is no glory in being a hotheaded martyr. And remember that Jesus died for the vicious men in the cartels just like he died for you and me. He loves them, and we can love them too. It's hard, but it's God's calling. Pray for your enemies."

Pablo began to advise the pastors in his network to pray: for Mexico, for the authorities, for the pastors, and for the people in the cartels. Another of his pastors was kidnapped and beaten very badly. When the thugs heard him praying for them and saw his composure, they were amazed, and they released him. Pablo knows that praying for enemies is no guarantee of peace with them, but it is the channel for God to give us his peace.

In the Bible, half the psalms describe painful emotions such as disappointment, discouragement, resentment, anger, fear, and depression. It's not off limits to be completely honest with God! But in almost all of these, the psalmist's honest engagement with God eventually leads to new insights, hope, and rest. That's the pattern of prayer for my global friends too.

Having a kingdom vision gives new energy, but it also creates its share of problems. People who relate openly and consistently with the public square and the community's domains take big risks and face genuine opposition. As NorthWood has shifted directions to the kingdom, the world, and the Holy Spirit, some of our families felt uncomfortable and left. We were becoming a church dedicated to God's kingdom, doing exactly what God called us to do, but our attendance and giving went down. Many people looked at our trajectory and assumed we'd missed God's will. I disagree. I believe God is very pleased, and he continues to open doors for us in the community and around the world.

At a mosque of twenty-five thousand Muslims, the imam introduced me by saying, "This is Bob Roberts. You have heard me talk about him many times. He's the evangelical pastor who is very conservative, but he loves Muslims. Because of his friendship with us, people have said hateful things about him on the Internet, and hundreds of people have left his church. But he still loves us." As I stood up, everyone began to applaud. I didn't know it, but that never happens in a mosque. What an incredible honor! I don't tell this story to pat myself on the back. Just the opposite. It's all about the wonder of God's grace to give me opportunities like this. If God can give this kind of platform to a roughneck from East Texas, imagine what he can do with you!

Pursuing God's kingdom has brought great joys and deep heartache. It's the way of the cross. Jesus came announcing the kingdom, and they killed him. Paul went into the domains of the Jewish and Roman cultures, and he was beaten in almost every city. When we follow God with all our hearts, our path won't be easy, but it will be right. On the way, we'll learn to pray like we've never prayed before.

Moses is recognized as one of the greatest leaders in all of history. But he didn't wake up one day and decide to lead the people out of slavery to the Promised Land. God called him. Moses hesitated and offered alternatives, but eventually, he obeyed God. He became a friend of God and an intercessor for his people. Time after time, he met with God, pouring out his heart for the people, pleading for forgiveness for their sins, and asking for wisdom, direction, and resources to accomplish what God had told him to do.

Moses didn't find peace, joy, and fulfillment in his calling. His purpose wasn't personal success and acclaim. His purpose was very simple: to honor God in everything he thought, said, and did. Moses never found happiness in his leadership and the response of his people; he experienced joy and purpose only in being a friend of God.

To extend the metaphor of the people of God in the desert, many Christians see their lives as journeys from one oasis of God's blessings to the next, and they believe the desert in between is an anomaly, somehow less than God's best for them. But all great stories, in the Bible and in all the rest of literature, are about finding courage in the deserts of life. That's where God first met Moses, that's where God revealed his glory to him, and that's where God provided for his people in miraculous ways, even though they doubted and even when they gave up hope.

Our prayers need to be much richer and deeper than "God, get me out of this desert!" They need to be "God, show me your glory where I am today!" When God revealed his glory, he opened Moses's eyes to see his goodness. The Scriptures often bring those two together: majesty and kindness, greatness and goodness, power and love. As we learn to pray, we need to ask God to reveal the full range of his nature in the depths of our hearts. And then, we'll ask God to use us to make his kingdom more fully realized on earth.

MY PATTERN OF PRAYER

I've noticed that many people are confused about prayer, but they're often too embarrassed to ask meaningful questions. It's my privilege to offer a little assistance. Actually, I feel that I'm only beginning to grasp the wonder of communicating with the infinite, sovereign God of grace, mercy, truth, love, and power. I've always believed in the power of prayer. Prayer has been and is a vital part of my life. I teach new NorthWood Church members and new Christians that it's critical to begin your day with prayer.

Prayer is spiritual breath. Prayer is talking and listening. Prayer is worship. For more than twenty-five years, I've begun almost every day by journaling what's going on, good and bad, reflections about decisions that need to be made, and my perceptions about life and God. Then I read three chapters from the Old Testament, one from the wisdom literature, and one from the New Testament. During my reading and writing, I sense God talking to me. I sing. I reflect. I worship. For me, it's critical to connect with God in this way the first thing in the morning because it prepares me for the rest of the day.

But my prayers aren't over when I get up in the morning. I pray throughout the day, I pray before meetings, during meetings, and after meetings. I pray while I'm driving, and I pray while I'm talking to people. In my mind and heart, I tell him, "God, guide my words carefully," or, "God, be present in this decision. Give me clarity." I pray nonstop, no matter who's there or what's going on, and I believe God hears all those prayers. There are so many dimensions to prayer; it's bigger than a formula, a set time, or a moment—it's a life.

THE POWER OF PRAYING WITH PEOPLE WHO AREN'T LIKE YOU

Many years ago, when I was in Afghanistan in the desert with some Muslim friends, they often stopped to pray. They laid out their rugs on the sand, and I waited in the SUV. But in a flash of insight, I thought, *I'm a Christian, I believe in God, and I'm praying too! I'll ask if I can join them.* At their next stop, I asked if it would offend them if I knelt down and prayed beside them. They loved it, and I did too. When we got back in the SUV, we had a wonderful conversation about the nature of prayer and how God guides us.

A few years later I was in Syria at an Islamic seminary, and I had the opportunity to speak with a group of people on religious freedom. At one of the appointed hours of prayer in the Muslim day, they went to the side of the conference room to pray. The Christians ate cookies and watched. Somehow, it just didn't feel right. I asked the Muslim leaders at the seminary if they would mind if I prayed with them. They said they'd be happy for me to join them. At the next hour of prayer, I knelt next to them and prayed. When we finished praying, some of the Muslims ran up to me and asked excitedly, "What was it like for you to pray?" I guess they didn't realize I've prayed all my life! My willingness to pray by their side broke down barriers and opened doors of communication. There were, though, no illusions. They understood they were praying to Allah and I was praying to the Triune God of the Bible.

Last year I was with a group of scholars and clerics in a Central Asian country. Each side explained their understanding of prayer, and then they prayed as others watched. At the meeting, papers were delivered and speeches were given, but the time of prayer was the highlight. Later, Doug Coe, one of my spiritual fathers, told me the pope was asking the leaders of Israel and Palestine to join him in prayer for that troubled land. Doug's conclusion was that the answers to the most intractable problems must begin with prayer.

Over the years, I've learned a lot about Muslims. In the early days, I viewed them as praying rote prayers like some Christian denominations do in their prayers, but that's not the case. They also pray throughout the day, about all kinds of issues and from their hearts. At a meeting of pastors and imams, we discussed the difficult problems of extremism, persecution of minorities, and how we treat each other. As we concluded, I told them, "Gentlemen, we Christians pray from our hearts. We don't often write out our prayers. I've realized that you Muslims pray that way as well. We disagree about the nature of God, but you are here because you want peace and you're willing to talk. Could we just join hands and pray from our hearts to ask God to use us to be instruments of peace? The message of Jesus is love, and the message of Islam is peace in its very name. Let's join love and peace and ask God to work in our lives. History is the story of God working through people, even when they didn't know it, so for the sake of others, can we do that?" We joined hands and we prayed together. It was powerful and moving.

The prayer meeting with the Muslim leaders led me to ask a penetrating question: What might happen if we prayed with people who are on the opposite side of an ideological, religious, racial, or cultural divide? What might God do if we prayed not just *for* our enemies but also *with* them?

I'm discovering God uses prayer in a way that revolutionizes relationships. How does that happen? Let me offer a few observations.

First, when a person prays, God hears. There is no "wrong time" to pray. God sees all and hears all, right and wrong, theologically accurate and inaccurate. He wants people to call out to him and seek him and his will. When we approach God with sincerity, he hears us. If we can't pray with people who don't believe as we believe, we need to stop praying with unbelievers who are sick in the hospital. I've stood by the bedside of people who aren't Christians to ask God to comfort and ease their pain. Yes, I try to talk to them about Jesus, but I'm still going to pray for them even if they don't believe in him. I've yet to have a single agnostic or atheist decline when I volunteer to pray for them. God doesn't go deaf and blind when we're with unbelievers. He hears our prayers for all people all the time—in restaurants and in prisons, in coffee shops and at political gatherings. Prayer was made for the public square!

Of course, some Christians assume you have to compromise your beliefs to pray in the public arena. You don't—not at all. No matter where I am, in America or on the far corners of the globe, speaking to Muslims, Hindus, Jewish people, atheists, or animists, part of my prayer states clearly that Jesus Christ is God and he died for all people out of his great love. No equivocation, no compromise; just real prayer to our great and gracious God.

Second, when you pray as a follower of Jesus, God is present with you. You are the temple of the Holy Spirit, and you can't turn the presence of God off and on. The Holy Spirit convicts and draws people to Jesus. When we pray, the Spirit is released to work in the minds and hearts of those around us. And the Spirit of God can go far beyond good theology or the latest practices in church growth. The presence and the power of God change people from the inside out.

What if prayer became central to our lives? What if we had more than token prayers at the beginning and end of meetings? What if we sensed the desperate need for the Spirit of God to come down on us, to give us his heart, his wisdom, and his power to accomplish his kingdom purposes?

And what if we offered to pray with our enemies, even if we have different views of God? What if we bowed our heads together, closed our eyes in humility, and asked God to work in us and through us to build new bonds of understanding? What might happen in us, and what might happen in our world?

It's time to find out.

I'm afraid most Christian leaders in America know very little about how to pray, and even less about the power of prayer as a tool of healing and reconciliation. It's time for prayer to come out of the church and into the street. God hears, God knows, and God answers. God is revealed—to us and to others—when we pray. I believe we've allowed the enemy of our souls to marginalize prayer, the greatest tool of evangelization the world has ever seen as well as the greatest tool of peace building the world has ever seen.

CONSIDER THIS

No one is limiting your prayer life but you. Some of us are desperate for God because we long for success or we want him to meet a particular need. But God wants us to be desperate for him because the kingdom is our mission. God will meet our needs, but primarily in the context of fulfilling his mission through us. When our mission is the kingdom, the world is on our hearts, and the Holy Spirit is speaking to us, everything changes. Our needs are no longer petty; we need God to do the miraculous! Our prayers are no longer tepid and superficial; we're filled with wonder, praise, and thanks because he has called us to be his hands, feet, and voice.

If our mission aligns with God's heart, we'll experience more thrills than we ever imagined and more heartache than we ever expected. We could say exactly the same thing about Jesus, Paul, and the other apostles. Prayer—real prayer—gets us on mission with God, and then prayer—real prayer—keeps us on mission every moment of every day through thick and thin.

Let passages about the wonder of God fill your heart, and then pray accordingly. After Paul described the sovereignty and mystery of God's grace to the Jews and Gentiles, he broke into what looks like a song:

> Oh, the depth of the riches and wisdom and knowl-
> edge of God! How unsearchable are his judgments
> and how inscrutable his ways!
>
> "For who has known the mind of the Lord,
>   or who has been his counselor?"
> "Or who has given a gift to him
>   that he might be repaid?"
>
> For from him and through him and to him are
> all things. To him be glory forever. Amen. (Rom.
> 11:33–36)

Don't settle for superficial prayer. Ask God to fill your heart with wonder and gratitude, and your prayer life will never be the same.

Part III

KINGDOM ACTION

Chapter 12

RADICALLY RESTRUCTURE YOUR CHURCH

I haven't written this book to excoriate the Western church. I'm not bitter, and I haven't given up on our future. Far from it! I believe God has an incredible plan for the church in America, but many of the pastors and church leaders in our country are mistaken about what it is. We need to open our hearts to God and our eyes to see what he's doing in other parts of the world. With a little humility and courage, God will transform our churches into dynamos of kingdom-building centers that produce multiplying disciples to have an impact on the public square and the domains of our communities. For that to happen, we'll have to make some important and courageous choices.

I started with a traditional view of how to engage the world: sending people and money to export all we knew about God in the West. However, as our church began to work in Vietnam, as I've had the privilege to know global pastors, and as I've worked with different state departments and nongovernmental organizations around the world, my perspective has changed—or more accurately, my exposure to all these people and domains has changed me.

As I've gotten to know the people in the Global Collaborative Community, our church has been adopting their emphases, their strategies, and their methods to contextualize them. We've begun to build multiplying disciples instead of putting our resources into a great worship service, we've begun training our people to minister where they live and work instead of primarily on our church campus, and we've begun to reach out to the leaders of other religions in our community instead of ignoring them.

In many ways the transition has been terribly hard, but it's been the most fruitful time of my personal ministry and the life of the church. Our church isn't huge or inordinately wealthy, but God has given us disproportionate influence around the world, especially in the Muslim nations. He has given us disproportionate influence in racial issues in our community, and he has given us disproportionate influence in the political realm because of the work of our people in the domains in our community and in countries around the world.

It's possible, it's really possible, to change the culture of a church, but it takes vision, tenacity, and dependence on the Spirit of God. The main points of this book can be injected into the bloodstream of the pastor, the leadership team, and the rest of the congregation. For some, this consists of minor course changes; for others, it's radical surgery. Here are my suggestions:

1. Establish family connections. God has given me a father's affection for my NorthWood leaders and my spiritual sons who are

leading other churches. To be honest, their church plants are doing much better at adopting the heart and strategies in this book than NorthWood because they can create this DNA from day one, while we're trying to conduct a more complicated transplant operation.

As I've watched people in our church and in my sons' churches make these strides, I've noticed distinct generational differences. Boomers and busters often have difficulty learning to see with new eyes, but millennials have little trouble at all. They instinctively grasp the concepts. In the past few years, we've lost some disgruntled (and often confused) boomers and busters, but we've added a lot of millennials.

We often talk about "the family of God." Some leaders have a tender, loving, strong parental heart for people; others (like me) have to trust God to cultivate that spirit in us. Whether it's natural or learned, pastors need to treat their people as parents treat their beloved children.

2. Make disciples the heroes. Turn the spotlight off yourself and put it on the people who are taking steps to reach out to the people around them—and those who are going to other parts of the world to be the hands, feet, and voice of Christ in the domains of other lands. As much as possible, delete the word "I" from your vocabulary when you talk about your church, and use "we" instead.

In every meeting, from staff meetings to congregational meetings of all stripes, put cheerleading on the agenda. And by all means, be authentic! Point out the people who are boldly, tenderly caring for others. Do your research to find out what kind of impact they're having, and tell compelling stories about their service. Make gratitude a hallmark of your leadership.

3. Redefine your small-group ministry. Small groups aren't a holding tank to keep people in the church. They can become hot-houses of spiritual growth—but only if the group leaders have a vision, a heart, and the skills to build environments where the Spirit inspires people and they gain the skills to touch others where they live and work.

Do a careful analysis of the groups in your church. How are you training leaders? How are the roles of apostles, prophets, evangelists, preachers, and teachers being expressed in the groups?

4. Equip your people to be effective in their domains. Small groups are a launching pad, and the church is the base of training and resources for all believers to be light and salt in their domains. The role of the church (and the role of the pastor) changes when everyone in the congregation believes God has sovereignly placed them in their neighborhoods and careers to make a difference in the lives of others.

But this perspective doesn't just happen. God has given us the responsibility to impart biblical teaching about the value of work, the credibility of integrity, and the skills to make a difference.

5. Connect your people to the world. Ask God to give you an open door for your church to partner with a city in another country. Look for ways your people can serve in the domains of that city. God has already given them skills and training to help there, and as they engage others in those domains, they can naturally talk about their faith.

You may already know leaders in other countries, and all it would take is a phone call to set up your first exploratory trip. Or you may need to dig to see what God allows you to uncover. No matter what it takes, trust God and make the effort. It'll revolutionize your life, your leadership, and the people of your church.

The emphasis on domains is effective both locally and globally. In the middle of NorthWood's transition, a young, handsome, successful Anglo couple with two beautiful kids joined our church. I asked them why they had chosen racially diverse NorthWood instead of a more homogeneous Anglo church. The husband smiled and explained, "We want our kids to experience all the colors and cultures of our society, not just one. The world is becoming more global, just like NorthWood."

His wife told me, "We love the fact that you love Muslims. We visited the Sunday the Saudi imams were here. I leaned over to my husband and whispered, 'This is where we need to go to church!' Our kids can be exposed to the world here, and they can see how to communicate the gospel to every person of every culture."

6. Open the doors for women in leadership. I know, I know. This is a hard one for some pastors and church leaders who are reading this book. I'm not asking you to go against your denominational policies or your theological framework. But I'm asking you to at least consider how to involve, provide resources for, and celebrate the role of women in leadership in your church. They see things men don't see, and they care in ways men can't fathom. Find ways to regularly get their input, and let them lead. Lean into inclusion. Your church will be richer, deeper, and stronger for it.

7. Rely on the Holy Spirit. One of the most important truths I've learned is that we're not alone. I'd been taught about the nature and role of the Holy Spirit, but I'm afraid it remained too academic for too long. In recent years, the Spirit of God has become far more

intimate and far more powerful to me—and far more mysterious in some ways.

As I've become more tuned to the whispers and shouts of the Spirit, I've experienced his presence and power in countless ways. All that I am and all that has happened in these years is a gracious gift from the hand of the Spirit of God.

MEASURING PROGRESS

If I measure success purely by attendance and giving, our transition to a kingdom-minded vision and strategy has been a mixed bag at best. But if I measure success by our ability to reach more diverse groups of people, build disciples who can truly multiply themselves instead of being content just to be in a group, minister effectively in the far-flung countries of the world, and trust in the Spirit of God to do the miraculous among us, then I can say we're making progress.

The process of moving from a traditional, American, mono-chromatic church to one with a kingdom vision is awkward and difficult. I have to clean up a lot of messes, and as we grow, we'll have to prune even the successes so we can grow even more. But I can't get excited about growing a big church when, as Hartford Seminary discovered in a research project with Leadership Network, only 6 percent of the members of megachurches claim to be new Christians. The other 94 percent represent "transfer growth" coming from other churches.[1] Is that really our definition of success? Is it God's definition?

As Brazilian church leader Robert Lay observed the Western church, he noted that we can't just add the kingdom, the world, and an emphasis on the Holy Spirit to our existing strategies. We need a radical restructuring, not a mild makeover. We need to unlearn as much as we need to learn, to stop as much as we need to start. We need to prune so we can grow something new and better. Some things need to die so we can truly live.

WHAT THE WEST OFFERS

Like no culture the world has ever known, the West produces a fabulous wealth of money, manpower, materials, books, training, and all kinds of other resources. From its inception, America has been marvelously pragmatic; we are can-do people who always seem to find a way to get things done. During World War II, the United States Army adopted a motto that perfectly states this attitude: "The difficult we do immediately; the impossible takes a little longer." The church in the West has this attitude too.

America and the American church excel in creating reproducible systems and models. We have brilliant, analytical thinkers who figure things out. We're incredibly bold, and we back it up with determination and skill. We determined to put people on the moon when no one had even been in orbit! We probably have more training conferences per capita than any society in history.

Another strength of the Western church is the separation of church and state. As I've noted, many believers in our country have taken this concept too far and live compartmental lives: sacred on Sunday morning and secular the rest of the week. Also, many Americans decry the erosion of values because of legal rulings and legislation barring prayer in schools, legalizing abortion, and allowing gay marriage, but we also need to look at the positive side of this equation. The church has been completely free from any bonds imposed by the government. The states and the federal bureaucracy don't appoint or control our leaders. We have freedom to worship, teach, and promote our faith in an almost unlimited way. In America, faith has had to stand on its own two feet in the public square or it would have withered and died. The separation of church and state has made us stronger.

JOINING FORCES

Paternalism fosters resentment, but humility produces bonds of affection and partnership. I asked Robert Lay how the American church might work more effectively with the global Christian community. He replied:

> Let's join forces around the strategies of the kingdom of God. Forget about nationalities. We need to think bigger than that. We're citizens of God's kingdom. Let's share resources, share wisdom, and share God's blessings. In God, we have far more in common than our differences. If we are open to each other, we can learn from the persecuted church in Indonesia how to live in joy and gratitude. We can learn from our brothers and sisters in East Africa how to live in harmony with Muslims. We can learn generosity from those who have so little but still give from their hearts. This kind of heart can teach all of us, including those in the West, how to live for Christ

whether we have plenty or little. Affluence has killed
the influence of the church in the West.

Robert has an interesting view of God and the American church.
He told me, "God owes America a revival because of all the good
things America has done for others around the world. Affluence has
killed the influence of the church in the West, but God will send a
revival." What will this revival look like? I think it may look a lot
like the examples I've seen in my friends from overseas. When will it
happen? Probably not until we start listening to them.

CONSIDER THIS

Some of you are church leaders in established churches, and some are
planting new churches. I hope the concepts and stories in this book
have given you fresh eyes to see new possibilities. The global pastors
have shown us a new day and a new way.

It's time for us to humble ourselves and pay attention to some
of the most remarkable leaders in the world. We need new metrics.
To uncover and establish them, we can ask the questions that are a
summary of this book:

- Are we building multiplying disciples, or are we
  focusing our resources on creating attractive per-
  formances on Sunday morning?
- Are we training and releasing our people to serve
  God where they work and live, or is their service
  to God confined between the walls of our church?

- Are we building relationships with the political and religious leaders of our communities, or are we ignoring them or complaining about them?
- Are we planting churches from the beginning of our church's existence, or are we focused only on building our own numbers, facilities, and reputations?
- Are we going to the world to invest our people and our resources in the global concerns of the gospel, or are our mission trips more like vacations?
- Are we trusting in the Holy Spirit's awesome power and life-changing purposes, or do we rely primarily on our talents, ideas, drives, and resources?

The pastors who have become my friends have taught me so much. When I think of these remarkable leaders and the people they represent, I realize God doesn't see a great divide between "them" and "us"; in God's eyes, his family is just "we." When Jesus prayed the night he was arrested, he asked the Father, "The glory that you have given me I have given to them, that they may be one even as we are one, I in them and you in me, that they may become perfectly one, so that the world may know that you sent me and loved them even as you loved me" (John 17:22–23). Jesus wasn't praying just for the American church or the Brazilian church or the Indonesian church, or for the Baptists or Pentecostals or Presbyterians. He was praying that all of us, of every denominational stripe and in every corner of the globe, would join hearts and hands—because we're all one in him.

ACKNOWLEDGMENTS

No book or ministry I've ever done has been achieved without the full support and encouragement of my wife. Even as I write this, she is in Vietnam teaching at the National University in Hanoi at an annual conference she leads on special education. She's been an incredible ministry partner, wife, and mother.

NorthWood Church is a rare church. We've had plenty of ups and downs, but we've never stopped moving forward. NorthWood is a church on a mission, pioneering into the future, into outer culture, and into the world in very unique ways. Our church has made my life rich, and I'm grateful for all who support me and the global, apostolic ministry to believers and nonbelievers.

Thank you, Chris Grant, who has represented me in every writing project I've ever done. You've been far more than someone who helps me get my books published. You've been a friend, a counselor, and a man of God.

Thank you, Pat Springle—where have you been all my life? You are an awesome writer. I hope we're just starting some fun stuff!

Thank you, Jim Peterson, for helping with this project. I like Anglicans a lot!

NOTES

CHAPTER 1: WHAT ARE WE MISSING?

1. "America's Changing Religious Landscape," Pew Research Center, May 12, 2015, www.pewforum.org/2015/05/12/americas-changing-religious-landscape/.

2. Kenneth Chan, "Fastest Growth of Christianity in Africa," *Christian Post*, February 28, 2005, www.christianpost.com/news/fastest-growth-of-christianity-in-africa-260/.

3. "Six Facts about South Korea's Growing Christian Population," Pew Research Center, August 12, 2014, www.pewresearch.org/fact-tank/2014/08/12/6-facts-about-christianity-in-south-korea/.

4. Wes Granberg-Michaelson, "Think Christianity Is Dying? No, Christianity Is Shifting Dramatically," *Washington Post*, May 20, 2015, www.washingtonpost.com/news/acts-of-faith/wp/2015/05/20/think-christianity-is-dying-no-christianity-is-shifting-dramatically/.

5. "Megachurch Trends," Insights into Religion, accessed February 1, 2016, religioninsights.org/megachurch-trends.

CHAPTER 2: A BIGGER PICTURE

1. N. T. Wright, *How God Became King: The Forgotten Story of the Gospels* (New York: HarperCollins, 2012), 161.

2. Cited by Dibin Samuel, "Mahatma Gandhi and Christianity," *Christian Today*, August 14, 2008, www.christiantoday.co.in/article/mahatma.gandhi.and .christianity/2837.htm.

3. William P. Blair, "Size Scales in Astronomy," Johns Hopkins University, October 2004, http://fuse.pha.jhu.edu/~wpb/scale.html.

CHAPTER 3: THE PURPOSE OF SUNDAY MORNING

1. Bob Roberts Jr., *Transformation: How Glocal Churches Transform Lives and the World* (Grand Rapids, MI: Zondervan, 2006).

CHAPTER 4: FAMILY CONNECTIONS

1. For example, see stages seven and eight in Kendra Cherry, "Erik Erikson's Stages of Psychosocial Development," About.com, December 17, 2015, psychology.about.com/od/psychosocialtheories/a/psychosocial.htm.

2. Anugrah Kumar, "Nearly Three in Four Pastors Regularly Consider Leaving Due to Stress, Study Finds," *Christian Post*, June 21, 2014, www.christianpost .com/news/nearly-3-in-4-pastors-regularly-consider-leaving-due-to-stress-study -finds-121973, cited in Samuel R. Chand, *Leadership Pain: The Classroom for Growth* (Nashville: Thomas Nelson, 2015), 213.

3. Chand, *Leadership Pain*, 212–13.

CHAPTER 5: REDEFINING SMALL GROUPS

1. Alan Hirsch, *The Forgotten Ways: Reactivating the Missional Church* (Grand Rapids, MI: Brazos Press, 2006), 15–16.

2. Henry T. Blackaby and Claude V. King, *Experiencing God: Knowing and Doing the Will of God* (Nashville: B&H Publishing, 2004), 121.

3. Lyle E. Schaller, *The Change Agent* (Nashville: Abingdon Press, 1972), 54–60.

CHAPTER 6: THE PUBLIC SQUARE

1. Andirudh Suri, "Why Is It So Hard to Start a Business in India?" Wharton School of Business, February 25, 2014, http://beacon.wharton.upenn.edu /entrepreneurship/2014/02/why-is-it-so-hard-to-start-a-business-in-india/.

2. For much more on the church's opportunity to be involved in social action, see *Generous Justice* by Tim Keller.

CHAPTER 7: ENGAGING OTHER FAITHS

1. United States Census Bureau, "Hall County, Georgia," Quick Facts, accessed February 1, 2016, http://quickfacts.census.gov/qfd/states/13/13139.html.

2. "Refugees," Encyclopedia of Chicago, accessed February 1, 2016, www.encyclopedia.chicagohistory.org/pages/1053.html.

CHAPTER 8: NO LIMITS

1. Wes Granberg-Michaelson, "Think Christianity Is Dying? No, Christianity Is Shifting Dramatically," *Washington Post*, May 20, 2015, www.washingtonpost .com/news/acts-of-faith/wp/2015/05/20/think-christianity-is-dying-no -christianity-is-shifting-dramatically/.

CHAPTER 9: ABANDONED

1. Notre Dame professor Christian Smith concluded that the young people of America have a belief system he described as "moralistic therapeutic deism"— beliefs they learned from their parents. See Smith's *Soul Searching* (Oxford: Oxford University Press, 2009).

2. Larry Crabb, *Finding God* (Grand Rapids, MI: Zondervan, 1993), 18.

3. For more information, go to globalengage.org.

4. Dietrich Bonhoeffer, *The Cost of Discipleship* (New York: Simon & Schuster, 1959), 89–90.

CHAPTER 10: THE NEGLECTED SOURCE

1. Daniel Yankelovich, *New Rules: Searching for Self-Fulfillment in a World Turned Upside Down* (New York: Bantam Books, 1982).

CHAPTER 11: PRAYER

1. Cited in Morgan Lee, "What Americans Pray For and Against (Per Max Lucado's LifeWay Survey)," *Christianity Today*, October 1, 2014, www.christianitytoday.com/gleanings/2014/october/what-americans -pray-for-against-max-lucado-lifeway-survey.html.

CHAPTER 12: RADICALLY RESTRUCTURE YOUR CHURCH

1. Scott Thumma and Warren Bird, "Not Who You Think They Are," Leadership Network/Hartford Institute for Religion Research, 2008.